GETTING TO

N⊘

HOW TO BREAK A STUBBORN HABIT

ERWIN W. LUTZER

David C Cook®
transforming lives together

This *Billy Graham Library Selection* is published by the Billy Graham Evangelistic Association with permission from David C. Cook.

A *Billy Graham Library Selection* designates materials that are appropriate for a well-rounded collection of quality Christian literature, including both classic and contemporary reading and reference materials.

David C. Cook and the graphic circle C logo are registered trademarks of Cook Communications Ministries.

The Web site addresses recommended throughout this book are offered as a resource to you. These Web sites are not intended in any way to be or imply an endorsement on the part of Cook Communications Ministries or the Billy Graham Evangelistic Association, nor do we vouch for their content.

Names and events in this book are the product of the author's imagination, based on his years of experience in a pastoral counseling role. Any resemblance to any person, living or dead, is coincidental.

LCCN: 2007934654
ISBN: 978-1-59328-186-1
Previous ISBN: 978-0-7814-4514-6

©2007 Erwin W. Lutzer

Previously published under the title *How to Say No to a Stubborn Habit* by Victor Books® ©1979, 1994 by Cook Communications Ministries, ISBNs 1-56476-331-5, 0-78143-882-9

The Team: Gudmund Lee, Theresa With, and Susan Vannaman
Cover Design: The Design Works Group, Tim Green

CONTENTS

FOREWORD

When Dr. Lutzer asked me to write the foreword for this amazing book, I was deeply humbled and excited to do so. You see, Erwin is one of the most respected hearts and minds in my world of books and radios. He is read, heard, and quoted by thousands of pastors who respect him as much or more than I do. But more than that, I am honored to provide the opening for any book that can help people find their way out of a tough habit or two or three, which is exactly what this book does.

Beware of what you are about to undertake, though, because it will not be easy. Most of the time, one sorry habit does not stand alone. It keeps company with other destructive behaviors that are designed for only one thing: to destroy our ability to feel good about ourselves, those who love us, and the God who created us.

Sure, there was a time when such things used to feel good to us. Why, isn't that the reason God gave us the freedom of choice in the first place? So we could do what we want, when we want to? Well, perhaps not. *The Message* version of Proverbs 14:12 tells us: "There's a way of life that looks harmless enough; look again—it leads straight to hell."

You see, life has many roads. Some of them seem wide and pleasant (the paths of least resistance), while others look hard and toilsome at first glance. And as we struggle with our various hurts, it just seems so right to take the easier way. But what few people will tell you is that once you are on this road, it can be very difficult to get off. Haven't you ever noticed how the expressway has fewer exits? Missing your exit may not seem like such a big deal at the time, but you soon realize you're in an unfamiliar place, miles away from your destination with no way to turn around.

At this point you must learn to make some difficult decisions. If you continue on your path (the expressway), the road will likely be smooth and straight. No one will bother you, and you can drive as fast as you like—at least until you run out of gas. But the farther you go, the more difficult it will be to find your way back. You may not know the side streets. There will be stoplights and stop signs and detours. Traveling down here can be slow, and it can be hard, but God never said this would be easy did He? Quite to the contrary, in fact, God tells us that change can be painful. First Peter 4:1 says, "So then, since Christ suffered physical pain, you must arm yourselves with the same attitude he had, and be ready to suffer, too. For if you are willing to suffer for Christ, you have decided to stop sinning."

That doesn't sound like very much fun, does it? You probably thought things would get easier when you finally decided to turn around. Well, be encouraged, because I actually think this is good news. Pain, you see, is a sign of progress. If you've ever experienced frostbite before, you know that the thawing process does not feel good. But pain, difficult though it may be, is a sign that the parts of you that were previously cut off are coming back to life. It's not easy to turn away from the pictures on your computer when you know no one is looking, and it doesn't feel good to curb your spending in order to pay off that debt. But such feelings are a sign that you've finally found the right path.

And what's more, we are not called to do this alone. Others have been here before, and can offer strength and guidance for the journey. We need those who care about us to help us do what we are not able to do ourselves. And that is where this book comes in. It is my hope that through reading this book, you will not simply learn what it means to defeat a habit, but you will learn what it means to join in fellowship with your fellow brothers and sisters under a common goal—to experience the power and love of God and the freedom the He designed for us. So welcome to a journey that will not be pain free, but one that will also be full of joy and victory. Believe me—it is certainly worth the wait.

—Stephen Arterburn

A HAND FROM HEAVEN

The philosopher Seneca cried, "Oh that a hand would come down from heaven and deliver me from my besetting sin!" His plea has been echoed throughout the centuries. We've all wished for the same miracle.

Stubborn habits begin innocently enough, but because we don't master them, they quickly master us. We all experience the cycle: enjoy a forbidden pleasure, feel guilty, determine never to do it again, take pride in brief moments of self-control, then fail once more. Each time we repeat the pattern the ruts are cut a bit deeper, the chain is pulled a bit tighter.

Excusing our behavior because "we're just human," we become pessimistic, even defiant, and soon find ourselves victimized by sinfulness that refuses to budge. This behavior pattern becomes so familiar that eventually we don't even want to change. As we settle into an uneasy smugness, we come to feel at home with our anger, lust, worry, eating habits, laziness, bitterness, and selfishness—except during our small and occasional attempts at correction. We may even begin to congratulate ourselves for these small bits of effort, though they result in no real lasting transformation.

Can we really be delivered from the one-step-forward, two-steps-back routine? At times I've thought the answer was no. Despite my sincere attempts at yielding myself to God, I've retained certain weaknesses (*sins* is a more honest word), which I've concluded I would simply have to live with. After all, *no one* is perfect!

But I knew my private failure was no credit to Jesus Christ, who won me to Himself by dying on the cross and offering me eternal life. Did He not promise that we could be *free*? Through many failures and a few victories I've discovered that the most persistent sin can be dislodged. We *can* be free from sins, even the ones safely tucked away in the crevices of our souls.

In ancient times, large cities did not exist with unending suburban sprawl as they do now. Rather, all the inhabitants of a city lived within the confines of a giant wall that served as protection from outside forces. Oftentimes during battle an enemy would concentrate its attack on the weakest point of the wall in an effort to bring it down. Enemies habitually exploited the same weakness—with startling success. Wouldn't it have made sense for the inhabitants of the city then to rebuild the defective fortification in preparation for the next assault? In much the same way, we repeatedly succumb to the same temptations without a constructive program for strengthening our defenses. We accept failure as a way of life, reasoning, "That's just the way I am."

God has a different plan—for which He has given us a message of deliverance and hope. True, there are no easy miracles. Our success is neither instant nor automatic. Slick and easy solutions lead to false expectations, which in turn spawn disappointment and unbelief. Applying biblical principles takes time and discipline. But steady progress is possible. Even long-established and sinful behavioral patterns can be replaced by wholesome attitudes and actions.

Seneca did not know that his wish had been granted, that God has come down from heaven to deliver us from our besetting sins. This book presents a step-by-step route to the freedom Christ Jesus has brought to us.

And if you haven't already done so, I would encourage you to find one or more people to travel this journey with you. I think you'll find there is no greater support than a fellow believer who has struggled or is struggling with the same issues, and who shares the same desire to live differently. The Scriptures tell us that "iron sharpens iron, so one man sharpens another" (Prov. 27:17).

To this purpose, you'll find a series of questions at the end of each chapter. These are meant to help you digest what you read along the way—either as a group, with a partner, or individually. If you choose to go through this book with at least one other person, you'll also find the short discussion guide at the end of the book helpful. In fact, you may find some of the principles helpful even if you work through this book on your own. Either way, I am excited to explore this path toward freedom with you, and I pray that you would be radically changed along the way.

And so, if you're ready … let's begin.

—*Erwin W. Lutzer*

Chapter 1

WHY SO MUCH TEMPTATION?

"Why is lust so powerful?" Taylor asked. The weight of his guilt was crushing. He had fallen into sexual sin. "How can I trust myself? I don't want to live an immoral life. I promised myself I wouldn't do this, but here I am *again*."

A woman, who for years had tried to quit smoking but always failed (regardless of the new remedy), once asked me, "Why is it that despite praying, yielding to God, and reading my Bible—why can't I quit no matter how hard I try?"

I have heard the same kind of questions from alcoholics and sex addicts who keep sliding back into the same destructive patterns of behavior no matter how many times they've dug themselves out.

Their questions deserve answers. Why is temptation so attractive, unrelenting, and powerful? Why doesn't God adjust the nature of our temptations so that the scales will be tipped more generously in our favor?

The Christian life does seem to be needlessly difficult at times. Surely God—the One who possesses all might and authority—could make it easier for those of us who love Him. So many believers succumb to one sin or another, often ending in ruin, so why doesn't God keep one step ahead of us, defusing the land mines along our path? If you are wondering how He could do so, consider these suggestions.

SATAN BANNED?

That's right—God could eliminate the Devil. In fact, had He done that at the time of creation, chances are that Adam and Eve would not have plunged the human race into sin in the first place. Most likely, our first parents would have obeyed God without pausing to consider the fruit of the forbidden tree.

Assuming Adam and Eve held the same free will that we do now, why didn't God give them the opportunity to choose without outside interference? The serpent was beautiful, seemed to speak with authority, and promised a better life. As far as we know, Adam and Eve had not been told about the existence of Satan, and so were quite unprepared for this abrupt encounter. If the serpent had been barred from the garden of Eden, Adam and Eve would have been more inclined to obey God. They might have chosen not to eat from the forbidden tree.

The presence of Satan in the garden, and his activity on our planet, tips the scales in favor of evil choices. I'm not saying we must follow his sinister suggestions, but if he were hidden away from our presence, we could resist temptation much more easily.

There's no doubt that much of the evil in the world, including our own struggles, can be traced to the interference of unseen spiritual forces. If God were to annihilate the Devil, or at least confine him to the pit, we could take giant steps in our walk with the Lord. No more one-step-forward, two-steps-back routine! Our battle with temptation would be minimized, and we would be more inclined to resist the enticement of sin.

So why doesn't God just eliminate Satan?

DAMPENED PASSIONS?

A second suggestion to minimize the daily failures of our Christian lives would be for God to dull the arrows of temptation that harass us from inside. James wrote, "The temptation to give in to evil comes from us and only us. We have no one to blame but the leering, seducing flare-up of our own lust" (James 1:14 MSG). Could not God dampen those passions to bring moral purity more easily within reach? Surely He could help us feel just a bit less tempted—just enough so that we would be more likely to be victorious and a credit to our Redeemer.

We've all heard someone say, "I know what I ought to do, but I just can't. I've tried, asked God to help me, and have still failed." Paul wrote the same about his own struggle: "What I don't understand about myself is that I decide one way, but then I act another, doing things I absolutely despise" (Rom. 7:15 MSG). The church reformer John Knox wrote these words not long before he died,

> Now, after many battles, I find nothing in me but vanity and corruption. For in quietness I am negligent, in trouble impatient, tending to desperation; pride and ambition assault me on the one part, covetousness and malice trouble me on the other; briefly, O Lord, the affections of the flesh do almost suppress the operation of Thy Spirit.

If this man of God had such struggles, is there hope for the rest of us? God could make it easier for us, but He has chosen not to do so.

REARRANGED SCHEDULES?

Even if God did not banish the Devil or dull our sinful passions, couldn't He guide us away from the places of temptation? Then we could be protected from circumstances that would provoke us to sin.

David sinned with Bathsheba because she happened to be taking a bath next door while the king was resting on the rooftop. Couldn't that whole mess have been avoided if God had simply arranged for her to take her bath two hours earlier, or an hour later? Surely a sovereign God would have had no difficulty in rearranging the schedules of His finite creatures.

Didn't Achan sin because he saw a Babylonian garment left unattended after the siege of Jericho? Didn't Abraham lie because there was a famine in the land, and he feared for his life? Didn't Samson divulge the secret of his great strength because of his attraction to the charming Delilah?

Clearly God does not shield us from circumstances where we are vulnerable to sin. Remember, it was the Holy Spirit who led Jesus into the wilderness to be tempted of the Devil. In the Lord's Prayer, Jesus taught His disciples to pray, "And do not lead us into temptation, but deliver us from evil" (Matt. 6:13). We must admit that God does at times lead us into situations that stimulate our sinful desires, but this is not to say that God causes us to sin—nor does He tempt us in the same way as Satan. Rather, these are the times when we must lean on God and ask Him to save us, when we are otherwise incapable of saving ourselves.

James wrote, "Let no one say when he is tempted, 'I am being tempted by God'; for God cannot be tempted by evil, and He Himself does not tempt anyone" (James 1:13). We cannot blame God for what we do. If we sin, it is because of our sinful nature; therefore we are responsible. But God does *test* us, and that testing often involves temptation. Quite unintentionally on our part, we sometimes find ourselves in situations that are an outward stimulus to sin.

Consider one married woman, who after running into a former boyfriend discovered that she was still in love with him. Consequently, she began to think she had married the wrong man, and felt trapped. She began asking, "Why did God, who knows how weak I am, allow us to meet again?"

Or consider another person struggling with homosexual thoughts and behavior. She admitted that her abnormal desires had begun when, at the age of twelve, she had a forced sexual encounter with an older man. So began a long struggle with sexual temptation. Could not God have protected her from this experience?

Another person, trying desperately to break his smoking habit, said that he was making progress until he was transferred to an office where everyone smoked. In an atmosphere drenched with the smell of tobacco, he fell back into his former habit.

Alcoholics, trying to stay sober, often slip back into drunkenness because of pressure from friends who do not understand the depths of the alcoholic's weakness. So it goes.

And what about the more subtle sins of the mind? Yes, Jesus taught that evil originates in the heart, but many of our struggles with evil thoughts are provoked by our environment. Those of us who travel don't ask for a room that has ready access to pornography—but we get it anyway. But whether we travel or not, all around us are stimuli that draw out the worst in us. Without taking us out of the world, God could lead us into circumstances less conducive to evil passions, covetousness, and anger. If at least some of the potholes were removed from our paths, the possibility of blowouts would be lessened.

But God has not shielded us from the places or the power of cruel temptations. Satan has access to our lives; our sin nature is unrestricted, and often without warning we find ourselves in situations that contribute to secret—or not so secret—sin.

Which brings us back to Taylor's original question—why is temptation so powerful?

SOME REASONS FOR TEMPTATION

A Test of Loyalty

As might be expected, God has a purpose in allowing us to be tempted. To begin, *let's remember that temptation, with all of its frightful possibilities for failure, is God's method of testing our loyalties.* We cannot say we love someone or trust someone until we have had to make some hard choices on that person's behalf. Similarly, we cannot say we love God or trust God unless we have said no to persistent temptations. Quite simply, *God wants us to develop a passion for Him that is greater than our passion to sin!*

Take Abraham as an example. God asked him to slay his favorite son. He was strongly tempted to say no to God. The altar he built was probably the most carefully constructed altar ever made, as he probably took his time with it. As he worked, he surely thought of numerous reasons why he should disobey God: Isaac was needed to fulfill God's promise. What is more, Sarah would never understand. And above all, how could a merciful God expect a man to slay his own beloved son?

Of course, you know how the story ended. Abraham passed the test; the angel of the Lord prevented him from stabbing his son and provided a ram for the sacrifice. Take note of God's perspective on the incident: "Now I know how fearlessly you fear God; you didn't hesitate to place your son, your dear son, on the altar for me" (Gen. 22:12 MSG).

How do we know that Abraham loved God? That he trusted God? *Because he chose to say yes when all the powers of hell and the passions of his soul were crying no.* This fierce temptation gave Abraham a striking opportunity to prove his love for the Almighty.

Let's return to some of those situations we mentioned earlier. What about the woman who seemingly could not resist falling in love with another man? Or the alcoholic tempted by his friends to revert to his old habits? Or the young man surrounded by the wrong crowd? Why does

God not shield us from these circumstances? He allows us the luxury of difficult choices so that we can prove our love for Him. These are our opportunities to choose God rather than the world.

Do you love God?

I'm glad you said yes. But what happens when you are confronted with a tough decision—such as whether you should satisfy your passions or control them? Our response to temptation is an accurate barometer of our love for God. One of the first steps in handling temptation is to see it as an opportunity to test our loyalties. If we love the world, the love of the Father is not in us (1 John 2:15).

Joseph resisted the daily seduction of Potiphar's wife because of his love for God. He asked her, "How … could I do this great evil and sin against God?" (Gen. 39:9). Even if he could have gotten by with his private affair, without anyone finding out, he could not bear the thought of hurting the God he had come to know. The same principle applies to us. Each temptation leaves us better or worse; neutrality is impossible.

That's why God doesn't exterminate the Devil and his demons. Admittedly, the presence of wicked spirits in the world does make our choices more difficult. But think of what such agonizing choices mean to God. We prove our love for God when we say yes to Him, even when the deck appears to be stacked against us.

What it boils down to is this: Do we value the pleasures of the world or those that come from God? The opportunities for sin that pop up around us, the sinful nature within us, and the demonic forces that influence us give us numerous opportunities to answer that question.

Transformed Passions

A second reason God does not make our choices easier is because *temptation is His vehicle for character development.* Sinful habits are a millstone about our necks, a weight on our souls. But that's only half the story!

These same temptations, struggles, and yes, even our sins are used by God to help us climb the ladder of spiritual maturity. If we see our sinful struggles only as a liability, we will never learn all that God wants to teach us through them.

There is a saying from Goethe, the German poet, that talent is formed in solitude, but character in the storms of life. God wants to do something more beautiful in our lives than simply give us victory over a sin. He wants to replace it with something better—with the positive qualities of a fruitful life.

Temptation is God's magnifying glass; it shows us how much work He has left to do in our lives. When the Israelites were wandering in the wilderness, God let them become hungry and thirsty; on one occasion they were even without water for three days. They became disappointed with their slow pace of travel; they were impatient with Moses' long rendezvous on the mountain. Why didn't God meet their expectations? Listen to Moses' commentary: "Remember every road that GOD led you on for those forty years in the wilderness, pushing you to your limits, testing you so that he would know what you were made of, whether you would keep his commandments or not" (Deut. 8:2 MSG).

There it is again—God allowed the Israelites to suffer temptation to test their loyalties and to bring out their latent sinfulness. Temptation brings out the best or the worst in human beings. The Israelites didn't realize how rebellious they were until they got hungry. Temptation brings the impurities to the surface. Then God begins the siphoning process. Sometimes God teaches us these lessons by letting us suffer the consequences of our own sin. James wrote that we are enticed by our own lust. That word *entice* carries with it the imagery of a hunter who puts out bait for wild animals, or a housekeeper who sets a trap for a mouse. The mouse sees no valid reason why he should not eat that piece of cheese. Since his knowledge is limited, he cannot predict the future, and he doesn't understand traps. So he eats,

and suffers a fatal outcome. Some of us, thinking we can predict the consequences of our actions, assign a more serious result to overt sins than to those
confined to thought and imagination. But even the sins of the mind exact
their toll, and ultimately we can no longer control the sin—it controls us. In
time God may dry up our fountains of pleasure and ambition so that we will
turn to Him in repentance.

When we do, God leads us to something better. He wants to develop
within us the rich character qualities called the fruit of the Spirit: love, joy,
and peace, to name a few (Gal. 5:22–23). God's purpose is to conform us
to the image of His Son (Rom. 8:29). To accomplish this goal, our character deficiencies (*sins* is a better word) must be brought to the surface so
that we can be changed.

God also wants us to humble ourselves by seeking others for help and
accountability. In the same way that a cut finger cannot be healed unless
it is connected to the rest of the body, we cannot find relief from our sinful habits except through community with other believers. Secrecy and
shame fuel addictions; only when we come to the light of God's presence
and the openness of fellowship with others can we experience the kind of
freedom we desire. Yes, we need the help of others. More on this subject
later.

Temptation always involves risk taking. The potential for devastating
failure is ever present. But precisely because the stakes are so high, the
rewards of resisting are so great. When we say no to temptation, we are
saying yes to something far better.

Strength for Our Weakness

Finally, *God uses our sins to show us His grace and power on our behalf.* The
depressing effect of sin is offset by the good news of God's grace. Paul wrote,
"When it's sin versus grace, grace wins hands down. All sin can do is threaten
us with death, and that's the end of it. Grace, because God is putting everything

together again through the Messiah, invites us into life—a life that goes on and on and on, world without end" (Rom. 5:20 MSG).

Paul was given a thorn in the flesh so that he would remain humble. Perhaps it was a temptation he struggled to resist. He asked God three times for deliverance, but God said, "My grace is sufficient for you, for power is perfected in weakness" (2 Cor. 12:9). Paul, therefore, boasted about his weakness, knowing that it provided an opportunity for God's power to rest upon him: "For when I am weak, then I am strong" (v. 10). If you are beset by an especially obstinate sin, you may be on the verge of seeing God's grace displayed in your life. Although you may now be preoccupied with your struggle, you may soon be preoccupied with your Savior.

God strikes at the core of our motivations. He is not interested in merely applying a new coat of paint, imposing a new set of rules. He wants to rebuild our minds and give us new values. The most important part of us is the part that nobody sees but God. And He wants to begin His work there.

Think about that one particular sin you struggle with most—the one that won't move off center stage in your life. Maybe it's an obvious one: drunkenness, drug addiction, or Internet pornography. Perhaps your imagination isn't suitable for certain audiences—or even any audience. Or maybe it's a sin of the spirit, such as pride, anxiety, fear, or bitterness. Whatever it is, God can deliver you from that sin. He can help you track it down and with the help of the body of Christ, root it out and exterminate it. Sin need not have dominion over you. You can be sure that God will never take from you anything that is good. Rather, when you are ready, He will remove the evil and replace it with something far better. He will tear down your fortress so that He can build an altar in its place.

Are you ready for such a transformation? The next chapter will help you answer that question.

QUESTIONS FOR GROUP STUDY
OR PERSONAL REFLECTION

1. John 3:21 says, "Whoever lives by the truth comes into the light." Take inventory of your life: What is your most persistent temptation? Be honest! Why is it so difficult for you to say no to this temptation and yes to God? In what situations do you most often encounter this temptation? What do you hope to gain from conquering this troubling part of your life?

2. Read the story of Jesus' temptation in the desert (Matt. 4:1–11). List all of the reasons why He might have found it easy to give in to Satan's suggestions. Speculate as to what the consequences of such an act would have been. Contrast His response with the way the Israelites acted when they were hungry (Ex. 16; Num. 11). What can we learn from this contrast between the Son of Man and the children of Israelites?

3. Before you read the next chapter, spend some quiet time in prayer with your own particular temptations or sins in mind. Ask God for wisdom in the following areas:

   a. to help you properly identify the cause of your defeat, and

b. to understand that you have been given the grace that is necessary to overcome this habit or persistent sin.

4. If you are reading this book alone, ask God to reveal one or two other people with whom you might be able to share your struggles, or even invite to join you in your journey through this book.

5. Take a few moments right now to thank God for the good things He is already doing in your life and for what He is going to do in your life, in particular how He is going to show His strength and grace at the point of your weakness.

Chapter 2

THE GROUND RULES

We are so desperate to change our behavior we'll try anything! Recently, I read that a drug company has been trying to produce a pill to treat addicted gamblers. However, tests have revealed that compulsive gamblers who took the drug did no better in curbing their gaming habit than a control group that took placebos. As of this writing, no drug has been found to cure people from the impulse of gambling, or for that matter, from other impulses that similarly destroy lives.

But countless people can tell how God has changed their lives—though He always does it on His terms. Before you can take steps toward positive change, You *must* accept three basic conditions. If you have trouble accepting any one of these conditions, you will continue to struggle with your unwanted habit or addiction. So what are these essentials?

BELIEVE THAT GOD IS GOOD

First, *you must believe that God is good*. Because of the evils that exist in the world, the goodness of God is one of the most difficult doctrines to accept. Yet, unless you wholeheartedly believe in it, you will be paralyzed in your Christian growth.

It is not surprising that Satan's first move in the garden of Eden was to cause Eve to doubt the goodness of God. Here are his words: "You won't die. God knows that the moment you eat from that tree, you'll see what's really going on. You'll be just like God, knowing everything, ranging all the way from good to evil" (Gen. 3:4–5 MSG). His point was, "God is restricting you because He doesn't want you to achieve your potential! You have the inherent right to be like Him, but He won't let you—He is selfish and doesn't have your best interests in mind."

Satan convinced Eve to believe that God wanted to restrain her from developing her potential—her godhood, if you will. Eve believed the lie.

Today, Satan uses similar strategies to dissatisfy us with God's will. Our anger at circumstances and our rebellion against God's commandments stem from our lack of confidence in God's goodness. The single girl seeking a mate asks, "How can God be good? If He were, He'd bring me companionship. Doesn't He know how lonely I am?"

The playboy reasons, "Why should God restrict me from pleasure? When I'm hungry I eat; when I want pleasure I should be able to have sex. A God who cramps my lifestyle isn't good. If He were, He'd have me find somebody who would really satisfy me."

The alcoholic complains, "If God were good, He'd give me a decent job. After all, wasn't it financial pressure that drove me to drink? Why doesn't God get me out of this mess? God is good? Good for *what?*"

I counseled a woman who needed to confess the sin of bitterness. Her response was, "If God loves me, why did He allow my parents to treat me like they did? A good God would never have allowed that to happen!" She couldn't forgive her parents because she couldn't forgive God for His lack of protection, so instead she chose to be victimized by her circumstances.

If you are a worrier, you also doubt God's goodness. You are afraid God will bring circumstances into your life that will be too much for you.

If you are greedy and covetous, you doubt whether God is being fair by not providing you everything others have and enjoy. If you experience uncontrollable anger, you are rebelling against God's will for your life.

Look closely at that sin you don't want to give up—the root of your stubborn insistence is a basic doubt of God's goodness. You do not trust Him to do the best for you, because *your way* is better.

Let's return to the story in the garden of Eden. Notice how Satan focused on a restriction and used it to blind Eve to God's blessing. Yes, there was one tree she could not enjoy, but presumably there were hundreds she could. Did Satan point out the many trees she was permitted to eat from? Hardly. He focused on one negative, and Eve forgot God's generosity and grace. So it is today. Satan will urge you to focus on one issue, one aggravation, one restriction. At that moment, he'll try to convince you that God's way is not best, but takes second place to what he can offer you … or what you can offer yourself.

So, I must ask, do you doubt God's goodness? Are you fully prepared to agree that His will is perfect and acceptable? If He did deliver you from sensual thoughts, would you feel cheated? If He denied you the pleasure of marriage, would you feel ripped-off? If you gained victory over tobacco or alcohol, would you be resentful because you had been denied this chance to feel good?

Perhaps now you are beginning to understand why you cannot begin to break your sinful habit unless you believe in God's goodness. The reason is simple: If you doubt God's goodness, you will only want to use God when you are in a predicament but keep your options open after things have returned to normal. You will be convinced that God wants to rob you rather than enrich you if He brings about permanent changes in you or your lifestyle.

I've discovered that the most frustrating problem in helping those who come to me for counsel is simply that most people do not really want to change. Of course, they are prepared to make minor adjustments—particularly if their behavior is getting them into trouble. But most of them are comfortable with their sin as long as it doesn't get out of hand. They would prefer to have God keep His activity in their lives to a minimum.

What causes this lack of enthusiasm for getting rid of sin? We are afraid that some worthwhile pleasure will pass us by. We question whether God's way is indeed the best. If we doubt God's goodness, we will not only resist change but will also fear it. A young man I counseled simply could not give his future to God for fear that God might require him to drop out of medical school. He doubted whether God's will for him would be the best.

Countless Christians resist surrender to God, frightened of what God might require of them. He might lead them to the mission field, let them remain single, or require that they give up their love of money or their pursuit of sinful pleasures.

When you doubt God's goodness, you hug sins tightly to your bosom, afraid that God will rob you of your crutch, your pastime, your pleasure. Occasionally, you are stirred to give up your sin, but you soon find you can't risk the loss.

But is your way really better than God's? Was Satan the good guy in the garden of Eden? And God the villain? Jesus put the matter straight, "The thief comes only to steal and kill and destroy; I came that they may have life, and have it abundantly" (John 10:10). To believe that your way is better than God's way is to take your place with Adam and Eve and believe Satan's lie. No matter how many pleasures Satan offers you, his ultimate intention is to ruin you. Your destruction is his highest priority.

On the positive side, if you accept the fact that God is good, two results will follow: First, you will realize that you can surrender to Him without reservations or fear of being cheated; second, you will thirst for change, understanding that the temporary watering holes of the world cannot compare to the everlasting springs of life that are in Christ.

So, are you prepared to yield yourself wholly to God without conditions, without reservations, and without a hidden agenda? No matter how attractive your sinful habit is, are you willing to let God teach you that His way is perfect? If so, you will be prepared to part with your sin, knowing that God will replace it with something better. You will have passed the first test as a candidate for radical change.

OWN YOUR BEHAVIOR

What is the second essential truth you must accept? It is that as an adult *you are fully responsible for your behavior and attitudes*. All of us are born with a propensity to avoid blame. Children display a remarkable ability to shift responsibility to others. My wife and I have observed that our children can spontaneously, creatively, almost ingeniously invent excuses for their misbehavior.

Because self-exposure is so painful, we become experts in self-protection, defending ourselves, tweaking the facts, and making ourselves look much better than we really are. This game of hiding ourselves from ourselves and the consequences of our actions is the result of being born with a sin nature, but it is inconsistent with what Christ requires of us as we are learning to walk with Him.

The blame game of hiding began in Eden. God asked Adam, "Did you eat from that tree I told you not to eat from?" (Gen. 3:11 MSG). The question was straightforward, and could have been answered in one word—yes. But Adam responded, "The Woman you gave me as a companion, she gave me fruit from the tree, and, yes, I ate it" (Gen. 3:12 MSG). What Adam really said was, "It's Your fault—I'm stuck with this weak-willed woman You created."

Notice Adam's logic. God created the woman, the woman ate the fruit, and then gave it to him. He believed that if God had not created Eve, or if Eve had not disobeyed, he would not have sinned. Hence, he was not blameworthy. In accepting responsibility, Eve fared no better. "'The serpent seduced me,' she said, 'and I ate'" (v. 13 MSG). She wasn't responsible either. Someone has well said, "Adam blamed Eve; Eve blamed the serpent; and the serpent didn't have a leg to stand on!" No one was responsible; it was God's fault.

But was it really? True, God created the tree, the woman, the man, and even Lucifer, who became the Devil. God could have created a garden without this forbidden tree and could have barred the serpent from entry. Yes, a sovereign God could have done it all differently. But *Eve made a choice, and so did Adam*. Thus they had to bear the full responsibility of their choice. The serpent also got his due—each made a choice, each deserved blame. In the garden, the matter of human responsibility was settled forever: Each individual must take responsibility for his or her choices.

A prominent American once said of Robert Kennedy's assassin, "I do not blame him, but the society that produced him." Will Rogers once aptly remarked that there are two eras in American history—the passing of the buffalo and the passing of the buck!

We cannot exaggerate the harm that has come to individuals from the teaching of Sigmund Freud that those who misbehave are sick. We do not hold people responsible for catching the flu, measles, or having cancer. We have hospitals, not prisons, for the physically sick, simply because they bear no moral blame for their illness. The reprehensible Freudian implication is clear: If people are not responsible for physical illness, why should they be held responsible for their addictive behavior? To say that a rapist, murderer, or thief is sick is to conclude that he should not be subject to punishment. After all, he simply caught a strange disease—he is the victim of forces beyond his control.

Recently, my wife and I watched a TV interview of a doctor who argued that the peculiarities of human behavior stem from the birth experience. If a baby is born in a noisy, bright, and seemingly unfriendly delivery room, the newborn will develop hostility in adult life. It follows that no one should be blamed for hostility.

If a teenager is in trouble, it's the parents' fault—they were too strict or too lenient. Or perhaps it was the teenager's environment—he or she was brought up in a wealthy home. Everyone knows that wealth spawns boredom, and boredom breeds crime. Conversely, the youngster is not responsible for inappropriate, self-destructive, or even criminal behavior if he or she came from a poor home—poverty drives people to drugs, sex, and crime. Even in a prison, it is hard to find an inmate who considers himself or herself guilty.

It is true that we are born with a propensity to sin. We are by nature "children of wrath" (Eph. 2:3), and therefore when we are left without restraints we follow our basest inclinations. But only when we realize our inability and need do we seek the attention of God.

Let's take sexual addiction as an example. One man, whose particular addiction had taken the form of homosexuality, once told me that his abnormal desires began at puberty, but not through association with a practicing homosexual. Rather, unhealthy factors in his home were so conducive to perverted thinking and behavior that this young man grew up believing he had been born a homosexual. In his words, he was "predestined to be weird."

Is it possible for this man to break free from his sexual addiction? Not if he blames his environment or his genes for his actions. This man did change. Listen to his words: "For years I believed that I could never change because I was a homosexual by constitution, not by choice. I took no responsibility for my behavior. But as I began to read the Scriptures, I began to believe God could change me. The first step in that direction was when I took full responsibility for my behavior. No excuses; no alibis."

When something is called sin, there is the possibility of deliverance—for Jesus came to call sinners to repentance. As Jay Adams wrote, "To call homosexuality a sickness, for example, does not raise the client's hope. But to call homosexuality a sin, as the Bible does, is to offer hope." Alcoholics are known for their ability to avoid responsibility for their behavior. Their spouse, their boss, their friends, or their neighborhood is to blame. However, the Bible teaches that each person is responsible. No one can make us promiscuous, or give us an ulcer. It is true, of course, that the abuse and betrayal of others can introduce us to sinful behavioral patterns. But ultimately, especially when we become adults, we must take full responsibility for our response to our past and our circumstances. And even in those instances where we are propelled by passions seemingly beyond our control, we still do the choosing. So we can still choose to let God have His way.

Of course, as I've already implied, we must be sensitive when speaking about these matters. Some people have suffered physical and emotional abuse, and therefore have reacted in sinful ways to cope with their pain. Others follow a life of sin because of the warped values of their parents. To some extent, we are all products of our heredity and environment. But even allowing for this fact, we know that a civilized society cannot long exist unless there is an assumption of individual responsibility for personal actions and reactions. We are all accountable, to family, employers, society, church, and ultimately to God. As a mature person, each of us needs to stop blaming and begin taking full responsibility for our reactions to our past, no matter how traumatic it might have been.

When we stop hiding and assume responsibility for our sin we'll find that we are candidates for God's mercy and power. A friend of mine put it this way: "God occasionally cures illness, but He has a sure cure for sin." Assuming responsibility also restores our God-given dignity. God did not create us as victims of circumstance, nor even as slaves to our genetic makeup. Whatever circumstances our pasts may hold, we can rise above them into a future shaped by God's grace.

Like Adam, who tried to avoid responsibility for his sin by telling God, "The woman You gave me …," we are all tempted to say, "The parents You gave me …" or "The friends You gave me …" or "The passions You gave me …" Many people have spent small fortunes on professional counseling when they could have solved their problems had they had been willing to accept responsibility for their actions and then subjected themselves to God's program for change as found in the Bible.

If we resist honest exposure, we will not be changed by the biblical truths that are intended to change us. The love and acceptance of God provides for us a safe place, where we no longer need to pretend and impress others. Because we are loved, we can be honest with who we are; because we are accepted, we can let God change us with the sure knowledge that we stand in desperate need of His help. The hiding has to end, and the fear of the truth has to be faced in the presence of a loving and caring God.

If you are still struggling, maybe thinking that I don't understand how badly you were mistreated or why your particular situation is unique, then you have probably failed the second test and are not yet looking for God to help you make changes in your life. Only the person who says, "*I* have sinned," reaches to receive God's mercy and grace.

TRUST IN GRACE

You have at least one more truth to accept before you can begin working on that stubborn habit. Quite simply, *you must believe that deliverance is possible.* To Adam and Eve, who sinned so flagrantly, God made a promise that Satan's power would be crushed when He told the serpent. "I'm declaring war between you and the Woman, between your offspring and hers. He'll wound your head, you'll wound his heel" (Gen. 3:15 MSG). The message was clear: In the conflict, Satan would continue to cause trouble on this earth until God overcame him once and for all through Jesus, the offspring of the woman. And now because of what Jesus has done, victory over sin is a possibility for every person who trusts in Him for salvation and deliverance.

The New Testament is above all else a book of hope. It details how God fulfilled this promise of victory. There is no sin—no, not one—that must, out of necessity, crush you. God has dramatically provided a way of escape: "No test or temptation that comes your way is beyond the course of what others have had to face. All you need to remember is that God will never let you down; he'll never let you be pushed past your limit; he'll always be there to help you come through it" (1 Cor. 10:13 MSG). In this verse we notice two facts.

First, you cannot plead that your case is unique or special. True, no two situations are identical, but your basic struggles against the passions of the world, your sinful nature, and Satan are the same as what others have faced. You can take comfort in the fact that you are experiencing a temptation that someone else has already dealt with successfully. In the Bible, Joseph did not succumb to lust; Moses conquered pride; Elijah overcame depression.

But what of people involved in the more stubborn sins of idolatry, adultery, homosexuality, drunkenness, or lying? The New Testament church at Corinth had these kinds of people—people who had been freed from their sin. In his letter to them, Paul listed the above sins and then added, "A number of you know from experience what I'm talking about, for not so long ago you were on that list. Since then, you've been cleaned up and given a fresh start by Jesus, our Master, our Messiah, and by our God present in us, the Spirit" (1 Cor. 6:11 MSG). Take hope in the thought that someone else has already faced and overcome your particular problem.

Second, Paul asserted that God would give you the resources to cope with temptation. A faithful God does not expect you to do what you cannot; He supplies the needed strength. Do you remember the story of the battle between the children of Israel and Amalek? When it was time for the battle, Moses said, "'Tomorrow I will take my stand on top of the hill holding God's staff.' … It turned out that whenever Moses raised his hands, Israel was winning, but whenever he lowered his hands, Amalek was winning. But Moses' hands got tired. So they got a stone and set it under him. He sat on it and Aaron and Hur held up his hands, one on each side. So his hands remained steady until the sun went down.… [After the battle] Moses built an altar and named it 'God My Banner'" (Ex. 17:9–15 MSG).

If you truly believe that you can't do what you should, then you need help from the people of God. You need someone to hold up your weak arms, to help you walk a straight path, to comfort you, to give you strength, to pray for you. However, if you say, "I can't" and let it go at that, you are calling into question the integrity of God's character or the validity of your own faith.

Why is it so essential for you to believe that victory over your sin is possible? Because *no one can win a war he or she believes can't be won!* To go to battle believing in advance that there can be no permanent victory is to succumb to the enemy before the campaign even gets under way.

Christians have often conceded to the enemy by assuming that some sins cannot be dislodged. Such unbelief breeds pessimism, disobedience, and despair. The teaching of the New Testament is that "all things are possible to him who believes" (Mark 9:23).

Name your sin right now and say, "Thank You, God, that deliverance from it is possible!" God has had a vast amount of experience in delivering His people from temptation—even from *your* temptation. Peter wrote, "God knows how to rescue the godly from evil trials. And he knows how to hold the feet of the wicked to the fire until Judgment Day" (2 Peter 2:9 MSG).

Are you prepared to believe that God is good? That you are a responsible person? That God can help you win victory over that stubborn sin? If so, then get ready, because God is about to perform a powerful work of transformation in your life.

QUESTIONS FOR GROUP STUDY
OR PERSONAL REFLECTION

1. This chapter identifies three necessary conditions you must accept if you want to say no to temptation and mean it. They include the belief that God is good, the understanding that you must accept full responsibility for your behavior, and the belief that deliverance is possible. Where are you right now with these conditions? What, if anything, is holding you back from fully believing these truths? See the following verses and meditate on their application to your life: Luke 1:37; John 8:32; and Hebrews 3:12. Seek prayer from others for your perseverance against sin.

2. No doubt David spent time finding excuses for his sin with Bathsheba. For example, unexpected circumstances led him to notice her just when her husband was out of town. God could have controlled those circumstances. Read David's prayer of repentance in Psalm 51 with these questions in mind: What evidence is there that David finally took full responsibility for what he had done? What evidence is there that David realized that sin is more serious than simply whether it hurts someone else?

Now read Romans 1:18-32. Trace the spiral of sin by asking, why is this man responsible for his behavior?

3. What do you think is the most difficult behavioral problem to overcome? Why do you think we so often fail in tapping God's resources for help?

4. Which biblical characters successfully resisted your particular temptation? Why do you think they were successful? Are there any people in your life right now who have successfully resisted this same temptation? If so, how can you gain their support and encouragement in your struggles?

5. Take a few moments now and thank God for the areas of your life in which you are already experiencing victory. Ask Him to help you remember those victories in times when you struggle with other areas of sin.

Chapter 3

PUTTING YOUR PAST BEHIND YOU

"For of all sad words of tongue or pen,
The saddest are these: 'It might have been.'"
—*John Greenleaf Whittier*

It might have been" has a way of catching up with us. We all know how painful regret can be. Regardless of how sheltered or permissive our past, all of us have at least one thing we wish we had done differently. "If only I had listened to my parent ..." or "If only I had chosen different friends ..." or "If only I had not gone out with that person ..." and on and on.

You must deal with your past before you can experience freedom in the future. The sin that troubles you today sank its roots into your life yesterday. You can't break your sinful habits until you have a new beginning.

Satan is particularly adept at using your past to ruin your future. His weapon is the illegitimate use of guilty feelings. Sins multiply in the soil of discouragement. One offense easily leads to another. You are caught in a vicious cycle until you realize that your past need not control your future. God promises a new beginning.

When I attended grade school in Canada, we often played "Fox and

41

Goose" on the fresh, clean snow in the schoolyard. After about fifteen minutes the trails would become so messy that we would move to a clean area and stake out new paths in the glistening snow. Soon we would have to move again, and then again, always searching for a fresh beginning.

I observed something at that time that stayed with me. Whenever we blazed a new trail, all of us children were anxious to stay within its bounds, but after the trail became wide and untidy, we were less careful about spoiling the pattern in the snow. In fact, after about ten minutes of rowdy play we didn't care how the trails looked. We even deliberately made the playing area as messy as possible.

What a picture of humanity! I think of a young Christian woman who expressed a sincere desire to serve God. Her way of life was prudent, respectable, and moral. But then, contrary to her intentions, she succumbed to sexual sin. She felt overwhelmed with guilt and the realization that she could never recover her virginity. Thinking that a new beginning was impossible, she threw all caution to the wind and sought sexual excitement with different partners. When this girl became pregnant, she did not even know who had fathered the child.

So it is with many who become trapped in one sin or another. Sinful habits have a domino effect. The common feeling is, "If I do it once, I might as well go all the way and do it as often as I like." That's why some Christians question whether God can change them. They believe they cannot live differently in the future because of the past.

Satan delights in this kind of logic. He wants us to think that we have gone too far, that since the past cannot be reclaimed, we might as well give up. James Stalker, the Scottish preacher, wrote, "The great tempter of men has two lies with which he plies us at two different stages. Before we have fallen, he tells us that one fall does not matter; it is a trifle, we can easily recover ourselves again. After we have fallen, he tells us that it is hopeless; we are given over to sin, and need not attempt to rise."

Stalker went to explain that both of these notions are false. *One sin does matter.* Even one fall can cause you to lose something that can never be recovered. An exquisite vessel can be broken and mended, but it will never be the same. Also, one sin leads to others. It's like climbing up an icy hill. Even as you attempt to rise, you fall again.

But when you do fall, you dare not accept Satan's second lie; namely, that there is no use in attempting to rise. Your enemy wants you to believe that since the past cannot be reclaimed, there is no way to break with its power.

Can you have a new beginning? In one sense, no, since the past cannot be relived. Virginity cannot be recovered; ruined health from nicotine, drugs, or gluttony may have to be accepted; a broken home may never be pieced back together. Even forgiven sin has its consequences. But in a deeply profound sense, you can have a new beginning. God offers two precious commodities: genuine forgiveness, a blotting out of all your sins—past, present, and future; and the assurance that your past need not control your future. The cycle of sin can be broken. You can rise again.

Listen to God's promise to an Israel possessed with violence, deceit, and sensual corruption: "'Come. Sit down. Let's argue this out.' This is God's Message: 'If your sins are blood-red, they'll be snow-white. If they're red like crimson, they'll be like wool.'" (Isa. 1:18 MSG).

Although a messy "Fox and Goose" trail cannot be straightened out, a fresh blanket of snow can cover it. The spoiled paths, the soiled places in your life, can be covered by forgiveness. Your blood-red sins can become as white as snow. You too can have a new beginning.

THE CONSEQUENCES OF GUILT

But to deal with the past, you must first deal with guilt. Feelings of guilt can be like a millstone around your neck, keeping you tied to your sins and wedded to your past failures. Sometimes your conscience may trouble you, rehearsing the sins of your past in vivid detail. Or you may just have a vague feeling of being condemned, a confirmed suspicion that you've blown it again and will always be a second-class citizen in the kingdom of heaven.

Living with guilt is like trying to drive a car with the brakes on. Guilty feelings can produce many serious consequences:

Physical illness is often caused by suppressed guilt. Some doctors have estimated that nearly half of their patients could be released if they could be told with authority, "You are forgiven." Christian psychologist Gary Collins has written, "The mere energy of keeping the guilt out of one's mind can put a strain on the body and cause it to break down."

Unresolved guilt causes depression. Feelings of hopelessness and worthlessness are generated by the nagging feeling that you've "blown it," and since the past cannot be reclaimed, there is little use trying to live a fruitful life.

Guilt is often the cause for lack of faith in God. First John 3:21 reads, "Dear friends, if our hearts do not condemn us, we have confidence before God." I've discovered in my counseling ministry that perhaps the most widespread cause of doubt is guilt. A person who feels impure will struggle with trust in God.

Guilt causes people to punish themselves. For example, some parents whose children have gone astray do not want to be free from guilt. They believe they must pay for their children's behavior, and that guilt is the price of the ticket. Others take this feeling a step further and interpret every tragedy as God's way of punishing them; some actually long to become physically sick so that they will have the satisfaction of paying for their sins. Such guilt feelings are never appeased, no matter how much they suffer.

Guilt often causes people to do good works. A husband brings his wife flowers in the evening because he has shouted angrily at her in the morning. Others give money to the church or are extra kind to a needy friend, hoping to atone for their sins. Some children who have rebelled against their parents become burdened for social concerns and even work in impoverished areas to try to make amends for their rebellion. Rather than ask their parents' forgiveness, they unconsciously assume that their sacrificial acts will balance the books.

But good works never erase guilt. Good activity can suppress guilt, can help you to deny it, or buy time with your conscience, but the guilt will soon surface in another form. A friend of mine says that it's like spilling ketchup on your tie. Resolutions to be more careful next time, or even the determination to become a self-sacrificing slave, will never erase the stain. Until a remedy is found that can be applied to the guilt directly, it is there to stay. Fortunately, God has not left you without hope.

PRINCIPLES FOR HANDLING GUILT

God's will is that you be free from all forms of guilt. He who is rich in mercy anticipated your moral and emotional entanglements. Fortunately, God is never taken by surprise. He offers you freedom from a nagging conscience. Let me suggest three steps toward finding this freedom.

First, identify the cause of your guilt feelings. This can often be done easily—an immoral relationship, cheating on your income tax, a harsh word to your parents—all these sources of guilt are quite easy to identify. Perhaps you will want to list these causes on a sheet of paper and then deal with each one specifically to put it behind you, once and for all.

Let me warn you that sometimes people experience false guilt, bringing torment upon themselves for matters beyond their control. A woman and her three-year-old daughter stood at a curb, waiting to cross the street. The child asked, "Mother, can I go now?" Absentmindedly, the mother answered, "Yes." Seconds later, she watched in horror as her three-year-old daughter was crushed to death by an oncoming truck. The horror of that event will never be erased from this woman's mind.

She is plagued with guilt, an incredible feeling of regret and self-loathing. She has not been able to forgive herself. We can, of course, understand her remorse. But there must come a time in her life when she puts those debilitating feelings behind her, knowing that they come from herself and not from God, who will not condemn us for accidents outside our control. This woman needs to forgive herself and to realize that self-incrimination is not what God desires.

To overcome guilt feelings, bring them into the open where you can deal with them. Ask yourself honestly why you are feeling guilty.

Second, realize that God's remedy for sin is complete. In Christ, God anticipated all of your feelings, discouragement, and failures. Jesus' death on the cross included a sacrifice for all our sins—past, present, and future. "Think of it! All sins forgiven, the slate wiped clean" (Col. 2:13 MSG). Every sin you will ever commit has already been paid for. All of your sins were future sins when Jesus died two thousand years ago. There is no sin that you will ever commit that has not *already* been included in Christ's death.

God does not find it hard to forgive. It is not as though He regrets giving you a second chance. The price for forgiveness has already been paid, and God wants you to accept it freely.

An atheist once asked Billy Graham, "If Hitler had received Christ as Savior on his deathbed, would he have gone to heaven, and would someone who lived a good life but rejected Christ then go to hell?" This was a trick question. It was asked in such a way as to make the gospel appear ridiculous. But the answer is yes. If someone such as Hitler accepted Christ, God would forgive him completely, because Christ's death is sufficient for even the worst of sins. God values Christ so much that He would accept even Hitler under the merit of Christ, but He would not accept even the cleanest person without Christ, for there are none of us who are innocent apart from Him.

Jesus' cry from the cross—"It is finished" (John 19:30)!—is but one word in Greek, *tetelestai*, a word used in business transactions. When this word was written across a bill, it meant "Paid in full." You need never try to make up for your sins on your own. Jesus' death paid for your sins *in full*.

When God forgives you, your sins are blotted out so completely that He does not remember them (Heb. 8:12). He never holds them against you again (Heb. 10:17). The sins you confessed yesterday will never again be a barrier between you and God—unless you refuse to accept God's forgiveness or doubt the value of Jesus' sacrifice.

I'm so glad my computer has a delete key. If I get my information wrong, or need to rewrite a paragraph, I simply press the delete key, the past is gone, and I get the privilege of starting on a clean page. That's what happens to your sins when God forgives you. The consequences often remain, but the guilt, the legal condemnation for the offense, is gone.

I remember counseling a woman who was living with unresolved guilt from premarital sexual experiences. Her guilt and subsequent unhappy marriage had destroyed her health. I asked her if she had confessed her sins of the past. "Oh, yes, I've confessed those sins a thousand times," she replied. "Well, has God forgiven you?" I asked. Her answer was, "I'm not sure."

What was this woman really saying? She was denying that God had included her sin in Jesus' death. And she was also saying that God was not faithful to forgive us our sins and cleanse us from all unrighteousness as He promised (1 John 1:9).

Why do people constantly reconfess the same sins? Sometimes, it's because they cannot believe that God would actually forgive so freely— surely they must suffer guilt first. Often they doubt whether they were sincere when they confessed their sins the first time. Or maybe they have never experienced grace and forgiveness from another person. Whatever the cause, as long as they feel guilty, Satan is winning a victory.

The Bible presents Satan as the accuser of the brethren. He brings their sins before them and before God during the night and during the day, but thankfully the redeemed can overcome him by the blood of the Lamb (Rev. 12:10, 11).

Satan delights in having believers reconfess the same sins. "Why don't you confess that sin again?" he suggests to our mind. The next day he tells us that we were insincere. "Confess that sin once more, but this time *really* mean business." And so it goes. If we fall for his deception, we are trapped by our own unbelief and become the victim of our own emotions. The result: no love, joy, or peace. We miserably sit on the shelf labeled "Unsure of Forgiveness"—a shelf already populated by scores of spiritually paralyzed saints.

And how do we distinguish between the promptings of the Holy Spirit and the accusations of the Devil? The Devil accuses us of sins that are already under the blood of Jesus—he accuses us of sins that God has already forgiven. The Holy Spirit convicts us of unconfessed sins that we must repent of so that fellowship with God is restored. But once we have repented and received forgiveness, the Holy Spirit has done His work.

How do you avoid this trap? The secret is to *thank God for your forgiveness even when you still feel guilty*. Use your guilt feelings as a reminder to give praise to God for His forgiveness. Memorize Psalms 32 and 103 and recite them with thanksgiving to God when those guilt feelings surface. This will become a great stepping-stone in your life, for you will learn to walk by faith, not by the whims of your emotions. And soon your feelings will catch up with your theology!

God promises you cleansing as well as forgiveness. Let's look at 1 John 1:9 more carefully: "If we admit our sins—make a clean breast of them—

he won't let us down; he'll be true to himself. He'll forgive our sins and purge us of all wrongdoing" (MSG). *Forgiveness* refers to what God has done objectively to restore us to fellowship, and *cleansing* is what God does to ensure that we know we've been forgiven. Or, to put it differently, cleansing is the subjective work of God whereby we are actually made clean.

A man struggling with Internet pornography once told me that even as he viewed the pictures, he confessed his sin—perhaps as often as two or three times a minute. But he discovered that, even after confession, his passions would continue. This is obvious proof that even confession in itself does not stop lustful desires once they are set in motion. But this man discovered the antidote to his problem. When he insisted, not merely on God's forgiveness, but also on God's cleansing, he knew he would have to turn off the computer. He said, "Sometimes I could feel the lust leave my body when I determined to accept God's cleansing."

By receiving forgiveness and inner cleansing, you can take the first step in putting your past behind you. Much more must be done, but at least you have begun the process.

Finally, pursue healing in all of your personal relationships. Many of us are in fellowship with God, but our consciences won't allow us to experience joy because we have unresolved matters between ourselves and others. These issues nag at our souls and remind us that not all is well in our delicately balanced psyches. Most of us, unfortunately, harden our hearts and simply choose to live with low-level guilt and inner irritations of conscience. Forgiveness and restitution is the only way to freedom. A telephone call or a casual meeting with a friend is often all that is needed to heal old wounds. But what if the other person will not forgive you? If you have approached him or her in the right spirit, you can be confident that God's grace will work its way in time, but until then be satisfied that you have done what you can to set wrongs right.

ACCEPTING GOD'S GRACE

God's grace is greater than your sin, whether the offense is big or small. A well-known Christian, driving too fast in the rain, caused an accident in which his companion was killed. Regret and the pain of guilt erupted in this man's heart. Yet he decided that he would not spend the rest of his life in the prison of self-incrimination. He chose to forgive himself, knowing that God had forgiven him. "That night," he says, "I saw more clearly than ever before that the purpose of the cross is to repair the irreparable."

John Newton had godly parents but was orphaned at the age of six. He was adopted by a relative who rejected the boy's Christian heritage. At an early age, Newton became an apprentice seaman. While enlisted in the Royal Navy, he deserted and went to Africa for one purpose—to sin to his fill.

He became a servant to a wicked slave trader and began sinning beyond what even *he* was comfortable with! Eventually, he escaped to the coast. There he attracted a ship by building a signal fire. Because he was a skilled navigator, he was soon made a mate on the vessel, which was making its way up the coast of Africa to England.

On one occasion, he opened the casks of rum on board and distributed the liquor to the crew so that all the members became drunk. As the ship made its way to Great Britain, it was blown off course in a violent storm. When the ship began to flounder, Newton was sent into the hold to work the pumps along with the slaves who were being transported. At that moment the faith teachings he had received from his mother as a child came rushing back to him, and he cried out "Lord, have mercy upon us!" The events that transpired on that day changed his life forever, and eventually he wrote those famous words:

Amazing grace! how sweet the sound,
That saved a wretch like me!

I once was lost, but now am found,
Was blind, but now I see.

If God is able to forget your past, why can't you? When you confess your sins and ask forgiveness of them, God throws your sins into the depths of the sea, and then puts up a sign on the shore that reads, "No swimming."

There is no reason for you to be trapped in the murky waters of your past life. God offers you a new beginning. Jesus said to the woman taken in adultery, "Go, and sin no more" (John 8:11 KJV). Once your past is forgiven, you are free from its grip. You have been rescued from the waters of sin and now stand at a fork in the road. With your sins forgiven you can either return to the slippery slopes of failure or plant your feet on God's soil, standing firmly by His side.

QUESTIONS FOR GROUP STUDY
OR PERSONAL REFLECTION

1. Psalm 32 is an account of how David felt when he tried to hide his sin. List the effects of unconfessed sin mentioned in verses 3 through 5. Have you been feeling any of these effects lately? If so, what can you do to change that situation?

2. Think of actions for which we often feel guilty because we cannot forgive ourselves. How can we know whether our guilt is brought about by ourselves or by God?

3. Reread the account of the fall of humanity in Genesis 3. What evidence is there that Adam and Eve felt guilty when God came to them? What characteristics of guilt are found in the record? What was God's response to their need? How can you relate to Adam and Eve's actions? How do you think God will respond to you when you come to Him with humility, seeking forgiveness?

4. Once we have confessed our sins, we must continually thank God for His pardon. Memorize these verses and recite them as an expression of

praise to God for His forgiveness: Psalm 32:1–2; Romans 8:33–34; 1 John 1:9.

5. Take some time now to pray and meditate on the times when you have not felt forgiven for your sins. Ask God to change your attitude toward His sacrifice, and to bring you to a place where you can accept His forgiveness and move forward. (Chapter 8 will further address how we separate our "feelings" from God's truth.)

Chapter 4

SEEING WITH GOD'S EYES

Are you still serious about breaking that sinful habit? Good. Let's get started. Since it is essential that you see your problem in perspective, consider the following stories. Perhaps you can relate to one of them.

At a young age Dave discovered that with the click of a button an entire world of Internet pornography was open to him. Years later, then married, he prayed to God for strength to overcome this addiction, earnestly pleading that his inappropriate sexual desires would diminish. He was submerged in guilt, fear, and shame because he couldn't resist the urge. Eventually his wife discovered the Web sites he had been viewing, and their relationship was deeply wounded.

Ken was a truck driver who promised his wife he would quit smoking. He decided to decrease the number of cigarettes he smoked each day until he was free from the habit. He failed so many times that he gave up. Today, he is convinced he can never quit and has no intention of trying.

Susan's first husband died young of a heart attack. Two years later she remarried. This time her husband was a Christian. After years of marriage to her new husband, though, she still longed for the intimacy she shared with her first husband. Ultimately she fell into an affair with another man. She prayed for hours at a time that God would release her from her desire to seek affection in unhealthy ways, but He never answered—at least not in a way that she could hear. Eventually the affair was discovered, and she and her new husband divorced.

John was a man with an explosive temper. Sharp words shot out of his mouth, shattering his wife's self-confidence and affection. He overdisciplined his children, usually in fits of anger. As a Christian, he knew better and even decided to change. Once, after a particularly sharp exchange with his wife, he put his fist through the wall. Humiliated and guilt-ridden, he asked God for deliverance from his temper. Vowing to change did not help; neither did praying. Months later he gave up, saying, "I can't help myself. That's just the way I am."

What went wrong? All of these people were Christians, all prayed to be delivered, yet all ended up more discouraged than when they began. The easy answer is to say, "They weren't sincere—if they had meant it, God would have helped them." However, many who are very sincere in their prayers—even to the point of genuine weeping—continue to struggle on a daily basis. Apparently sincerity in itself doesn't guarantee deliverance.

One reason people revert to their old behavior patterns is that *they misunderstand the full extent of their problem.* True, they want victory, but they don't understand how or why God will bring it about. Like them, most of us want to overcome a specific habit—for our own benefit. We want to be free of the symptoms of a problem, but avoid a thorough examination that might reveal deeper problems in our lives, which we are unwilling to face. Habits themselves are like the tip of an iceberg, with 90 percent of the issue usually lying deeper under the surface. Let me explain.

Dave wanted to break his pornography habit because he felt guilty; furthermore, he lived in constant fear of being discovered. He sought God's assistance to save his marriage and, above all, his reputation. This, of course, is understandable; we can all identify with such motivation. But his life needed many other adjustments.

First of all, he was selfish, spending much of his free time working on cars. He considered his family an inconvenience. How can we expect to defeat a habit if we cannot first put others before ourselves? Second, he was prideful. Dave and his wife would often get into arguments, which he turned into opportunities to blame her for the circumstances in his life. He would rationalize that she didn't care about him enough—in fact, she was probably the reason this stubborn habit still existed in his life, though he knew well enough that this sin had existed in his life long before he ever met her.

What was God's concern for this man? That he stop viewing pornography and lusting after women who were not his wife? Yes. But God wanted much more than that for Dave. God wanted him to humble himself, to ask the forgiveness of his wife and children, to reorganize his priorities. Dave needed to connect with other Christian men who would be honest with him and hold him accountable. He had some bad attitudes he needed to confess, pride that he needed to break, and selfishness he needed to face head-on. More important, he needed to put God first in his life. But Dave wasn't concerned about such drastic treatment. God wanted to take charge of Dave's entire house, but Dave just wanted Him to sweep the front steps.

And what about Ken? He wanted to quit smoking. Yes, he was a Christian, but he lived only on the fringes of spiritual commitment. His children had never heard him pray, except for the perfunctory grace said at mealtimes. He was not a spiritual leader in his home; his wife taught the children the few Bible stories they knew.

Now he wanted God to help him quit smoking because the doctors told him he might die of lung cancer. Could God help him overcome that habit? Yes indeed. But he would have to yield himself fully to God—his time, property, and reputation would have to be committed to the Almighty. Ken would have to begin reading the Scriptures and turning to

God daily for his own needs and the needs of his family. But he didn't bargain for such changes. He thought God would deliver him from cigarettes and leave the rest of his life untouched.

And why didn't God deliver Susan from her perceived needs? Deep within, she faced long-standing struggles related to her first marriage that she had never resolved. She was also nervous and fearful, and had a history of nagging her husband and children about almost everything. Her present situation was inflamed with self-pity—one sin she was not prepared to part with. She continually justified her attitudes, extolling her own righteous behavior, and bemoaning the fact that she, of all people, had been so sorely mistreated by the loss of her first husband.

We can sympathize with her. Her emotional anguish was enormous, even beyond description. But the fact remains that self-pity cannot be defeated until we take ownership of our behavior. For many people, even prayer itself becomes another self-pitying session in which God is informed—even blamed—in meticulous detail for all wrongs suffered.

Finally, there is John. He thought he was simply born with a short fuse. And of course, his circumstances were to blame—if everything would go more to his liking, there would be no need to blow up, no need to put his fist through the wall. Actually, John is always angry—angry at his employer, angry at life itself. He feels unworthy because he never became the success his absentee father hoped he would be. He will have to face the feelings of rejection he suffered in his childhood and submit them to God for emotional healing—forgiveness will have to replace resentment.

Though John doesn't realize it, he is a man at war with God, rebelling against the vocation and the circumstances of life to which God has called him. Until he accepts himself and his place in the world with joyful thanksgiving, he will never learn to control his temper. God is concerned about changing these attitudes, but John isn't. He wants victory over his temper to avoid future embarrassment and to keep his marriage intact. He wants the minimum required to maintain his life on a fairly even keel—but no more.

FACE THE ISSUES

How easy it is to seek freedom from a particular sin without facing basic issues! One day, a man who had been fired from his job called me on the phone. I had never met him, but he asked me what he could do to develop his willpower. He simply could not get to work on time and had been fired from two previous jobs because of his laziness and lack of punctuality. I gave him some suggestions, hoping to help him.

A week later, I received a phone call from a woman seeking advice on how to end an illicit sexual affair. To my chagrin, the man she was involved with was the one I had spoken to a week earlier! His problem of sensuality had affected all areas of his life. How accurate James was when he taught that a double-minded man is unstable in *all* his ways (James 1:8).

Sinful habits are usually indicative of unresolved conflicts. We must always look for underlying causes rather than just treat the symptoms. God uses our struggles with sin to diagnose our true condition. Temptation is His X-ray machine, revealing the hidden conflicts that need attention.

WHAT DOES GOD WANT TO ACCOMPLISH?

God has a larger purpose in wanting to show us our inner self. Unfortunately, we too often seek the smaller purpose: We desire freedom from sin to avoid embarrassment, to be relieved of guilt, or to save a marriage. However, the deeper issue we often avoid is our rebellion against God. A man may be dishonest in business; a woman may have had an abortion—both may want to be free from a nagging conscience, but they may not be willing to deal with their basic attitude of defiance of God's authority.

Genuine repentance is never easy. To confess our sins means that we agree with God that we have sinned; it also means that we agree that the sin must be forsaken. Those who confess their sins, intending to repeat the same action, are only partially repentant—if at all. Such incomplete repentance leads to a downward spiral of repeated failure. Confession means that we admit our sin and give God permission to remove it from our life. Of course, I'm not saying that we will never commit the same sin again—if so, none of us could claim forgiveness. But there needs to be a willingness to part with sin, and a submission to God's verdict on the matter. Apart from such an acknowledgment, our intentions are self-centered. We are inquiring how forgiveness will benefit us instead of considering how we have offended God.

So, confess your sins to God and repent of them. But don't stop there. God wants to draw you beyond repentance to Himself. He wants to use your struggles to lead you into godly living. His will is not merely that you be free from sin; He wants to conform you to the image of His Son. Delivering you from sinful habits is only a step in the process. Washing the stains from your life is His prelude to changing you into the Spirit-filled person He wants you to be.

A young man, caught in the grip of homosexuality, struggled with this sin for a period of years. But God eventually changed him so radically that he developed normal attractions for the opposite sex. Today he is a godly, sensitive young man. God taught him principles of commitment that he has been able to apply to all areas of his life. He memorized more than two hundred verses of Scripture during those months of agonizing struggle. His sinful habit drove him to become intimately acquainted with the Almighty and His Word. He once was occupied with his problem; today he is occupied with his Provider.

When you are faced with excruciating temptation, you have a choice to make. You can say: "I've tried to change before, and it hasn't worked, so

I'll manage the best I can with my sin. We're all human, you know." And your sin will be a monument to the false god you have fashioned.

Or, you can take a look at your sinful habit and see it as a challenge to display God's grace and power in your life. To the scattered Jewish Christians, James wrote, "Consider it all joy, my brethren, when you encounter various trials, knowing that the testing of your faith produces endurance. And let endurance have its perfect result, that you may be perfect and complete, lacking in nothing" (James 1:2–4).

God does not make special deliveries of spiritual victory to just anyone who requests them. Your sin cost Him the life of His Son; He is not about to hand out a spiritual Band-Aid to hide a spiritual cancer. But God will use your struggles to give you a thorough housecleaning, reorganize your priorities, and make you dependent on His grace. There are no cheap, easy miracles. You must want spiritual freedom, not merely for your own sake, but for God's sake as well. Only then will you find the victory He promises.

GETTING A LARGER FOCUS

There is a difference between temptation and sin. Choosing to pursue the temptation is sin, but the temptation itself isn't. Even our Lord was tempted (Heb. 4:15).

When sinful thoughts enter your mind, unwelcome and without fanfare, at that point you have not sinned. But then the crucial test comes: How will you respond to such suggestions? Will you pursue these thoughts, entertain them, and let them be at home in your mind?

Many Christians think that victory over sin means that they will no longer be tempted. Or they think that God will change their nature so that they will no longer desire to do evil. Either way, they are wrong. Temptation is not a sin; it is a call to battle.

I remember my own struggles with sinful lusts, as I implored God to deliver me from these passions. I expected God to change my desires so that I would no longer be stimulated when temptations came my way. Needless to say, I was disappointed. God does not change our nature so that we are less than human. Temptation of one kind or another is universal. To pray that we will no longer be tempted is to ask that we die and go to heaven. Since we will always be tempted, we need to learn to handle temptation in God's way. Here are several steps to ensure that you are dealing with temptation in a godly manner.

First, thank God for temptations and the opportunities they represent in your life. Each temptation gives you a clear-cut opportunity to declare your allegiance to Jesus Christ. Persistent praise is the first positive step toward overcoming temptation. God is glorified when you accept your circumstances as from His hand. If you cannot thank God for your condition and even your temptation, you are rebelling against Him. A man wrestling with a fierce temptation once told me he could not resist it until he gave thanks to God continually for his struggle. "Lord," he prayed, "I thank You for this temptation; even if I should be tempted from now until the day I die, I give thanks for it."

The first step in seeing from God's perspective. Accept the fact that you will be tempted; then choose to thank God for the opportunity it represents.

Second, spend some time defining your basic attitudes. Take a tour through your life and jot down areas that need work. What is it that *really* bothers you? What do you really want? Are you rebelling against some person? Are you upset with your performance? Your appearance? Do you feel like a failure? Do you think that you have been shortchanged since becoming a Christian? Are you bitter toward your parents, children, husband, or wife? Are you angry at God because He hasn't done what you think He ought? Spend an hour taking inventory.

Whenever I do so, I always discover attitudes I didn't know I had. For example, I'm often upset with myself because it takes me so long to accomplish a project—writing a book, for instance. I'm preoccupied with struggles in the ministry, frustration in personal relationships, and responsibilities as a husband, father, and grandfather. All of this affects my attitude, my perspective. God has been showing me that the way I handle these attitudes will affect my relationship with Him and will bring either honor or dishonor to His name.

Third, after you have had time to reflect on your private struggles, give yourself and your problem completely to God. Give God the key to every room in your soul and let Him enter and take charge. Do so knowing that God will require you to deal with those attitudes and sins you have so carefully justified. This may be a long and painful process, but it can be lastingly beneficial.

But don't be afraid of what God might demand of you. A woman who was very shy and withdrawn once told me she was afraid to give herself to God because she might have to learn to be friendly. Undoubtedly you will face some difficult situations, especially those in which you will have to ask forgiveness of others. Some situations will even require the guidance of a biblical counselor. But I think you will find that the pain is worth it, as God works all things together for good in your life (Rom. 8:28).

And whatever God asks of you, He will give you the strength to do. Perhaps you have come to a stream where the bridge has washed away—it still may be possible to cross it, though not in short steps. Now is the time for you to leap! So it is when you give yourself to God. When the bridge of blame and excuses is gone, take that one long jump without any thought of returning to a life of halfhearted commitment. Though your dedication may have to be renewed many times, make it as clear, specific, and final as you can, knowing God will be with you to keep you walking in His way.

Finally, realize that your ultimate goal is not victory, but relationship with God Himself. Augustine wrote in his *Confessions,* "O Lord, Thou hast made us for Thyself, and our hearts are restless until they find their all in Thee." Ultimately, not even victory over sin can satisfy our innermost desires. Only God can meet our deepest needs, for He has created us as social creatures, and we must be in relationship with Him to realize our full potential as His children.

Let me be perfectly clear here: Surrender is but the first step of a long process. Hearts are changed the moment they accept Christ, but much more work is needed to change the thoughts and attitudes of the mind and the habits of the body.

Remember Copernicus? He was the astronomer who concluded that the earth rotated around the sun, and not vice versa. With the sun at the center of the universe, the planetary motion could be explained more easily. The complicated equations needed to explain the movement of the planets were simplified by this new theory.

God wants you to have your own Copernican revolution. He longs to be made the very center of your life—to reward you and bring your life meaning through serving the Sovereign who is both Creator and Redeemer. The victory over sin that you seek will come from your relationship with God. When you seek to know God and love Him with your whole mind, heart, and soul, the freedom you are looking for will become yours.

You may think that knowing God is a rather theoretical and mystical goal. God is invisible, and may seem inaccessible. Isn't it easier to establish goals in business or in your marriage and family life? The wonderful promise of the Scriptures is that you *can* know God. To the prophet Jeremiah God said, "When you call on me, when you come and pray to me, I'll listen. When you come looking for me, you'll find me. Yes, when you get serious about finding me and want it more than anything else, I'll make sure you won't be disappointed" (Jer. 29:12–14 MSG).

Throughout the Bible, the desire to know God is compared to a thirst. The Old Testament prophets spoke of the time when the land would be flowing with water, when God Himself would give His people springs in the desert. Jesus spoke of Himself as the One who could provide living water. He said, "If anyone thirsts, let him come to me and drink. Rivers of living water will brim and spill out of the depths of anyone who believes in me this way" (John 7:37–38 MSG).

Are you thirsty for this living water, water that can satisfy the innermost reaches of your soul? Perhaps you can relate to this poem from Nancy Spiegelberg:

> *Lord,*
> *I crawled*
> *across the barrenness*
> *to You*
> *with my empty cup,*
> *uncertain*
> *in asking*
> *any small drop*
> *Of refreshment.*
>
> *If only*
> *I had known You better*
> *I'd have come*
> *Running*
> *With a bucket*

The better you know God, the more often you will turn to Him. The more you understand that you are created for fellowship with Him, the more time you will spend fulfilling that purpose, until your life demonstrates the singleness of devotion that Paul expressed: "This one thing I do" (Phil. 3:13 KJV).

When you come to see yourself and your life from God's perspective, you will learn to pray optimistically and in faith. God has brought this temptation to you for your good. Now thank Him for how He will use it. He wants to build and not to destroy. If He wounds you, it is so that He might heal you in the depths of your being.

If you are serious about breaking that sinful habit, why not pray right now, thanking God for what He will do in your life?

> *Lord, I confess my sin, particularly my rebellion against Your authority. In agreeing that I have sinned, I also agree that this sin must be forsaken. Thank You for Your forgiveness. I am grateful for this powerful temptation, which gives me the chance to prove that I love You more than any pleasure in the world. I thank You that the temptation is not greater than I can bear, and I rejoice at how You will use it in my life. I look forward to getting to know You better, and I am glad that You have sent me this trial as a reminder of how desperately I need You. Help me to remember to give thanks at all times and in all circumstances.*
>
> *In Jesus' name, amen.*

QUESTIONS FOR GROUP STUDY
OR PERSONAL REFLECTION

1. Most of our repeated failures stem from one of three basic causes: (a) pride, (b) sensuality, or (c) covetousness. Read Genesis 3:1–8 and try to find these three elements in Satan's temptation of Adam and Eve.

2. Try to relate your particular temptation to one or more of the root problems mentioned above. For example: the sin of anger actually reflects pride and an unwillingness to forgive those who have wronged us. Our expected struggles with lust are enflamed by pornography when we believe that these pleasures outweigh the benefits of obedience to God.

3. Think of some Bible characters who tried to cover or excuse their sin. What was the result for them personally, and for other people?

4. Take Paul's list of the works of the flesh found in Galatians 5:19–21, and describe the way in which each one is symptomatic of rebellion against God.

5. In thinking of the particular sin you would like to overcome, ask yourself: *What would God want to put in the place of this habit?* Read the Beatitudes and find the character qualities that seem to be directly opposite of the trait you want God to change (Matt. 5:1–11). Now spend some time in prayer and ask God to use your particular temptation as a tool to mold your character into what He would have it become.

Chapter 5

THE FREEDOM OF LIVING AT THE CROSS

When you try to break a sinful habit or thought pattern, you discover that the chains of habit have rested so lightly that you didn't even feel them until now, when they are so strong that you are unable to break them. Sin does not appear to be irresistible—until you want to be free from it. The moment you attack it, you are surprised to find that it is strong. You feel like the man who tried to drain a swamp, not knowing it was fed by an underground stream.

You have already read illustrations of people who were overcome by sinful passions. Your immediate response might be to launch an assault on these habits, learn to curb them, and develop enough fortitude to say no to sinful impulses. But the end result will be discouragement and bitter disappointment because you will be dealing with external behavior rather than with the core of your motivations. You'll be draining the swamp, but not stopping the underground supply.

FINDING THE SOURCE

Did you know that all sinful habits have a common source? We have a tendency to think of some sins as "less sinful" than others. A man might remark self-righteously, "I have a bad temper, but you'll never catch me drunk." Or a woman might say, "I do struggle with covetousness and discontent, but I'd never commit adultery."

It is true that some sins do have worse consequences than others. The thoughts of lust and hatred do not lead to the same social consequences as the acts of adultery and murder. In this sense all sins are not the same. But from another perspective, all sins are essentially the same because they originate from the same source. We can't rate sins on a scale somewhere between serious and minor. Some sins may be trifling to us but not to God. The reason: all sins originate from the corruption of our rebellious sinful nature. The New Testament writers often referred to this sinful nature as "the flesh."

Perhaps you are wondering what the "flesh" is. The "flesh" is a compulsive inner force inherited from man's fall that expresses itself in general and specific rebellion against God. In spiritual terms it is what is often called the "self," referring to the incurable desire to put personal interests above God's. More particularly, it manifests as pride, sensuality, and covetousness. By nature, we meticulously protect our reputations, we yield to the lusts of the body, and we desire to possess things and people so that our confidence need not be in God.

Read these verses carefully. Do you see the consequences of your own personal sin listed here?

> It is obvious what kind of life develops out of trying to get your own way all the time: repetitive, loveless, cheap sex; a stinking accumulation of mental and emotional garbage; frenzied and joyless grabs for happiness; trinket gods; magic-show religion; paranoid loneliness; cutthroat competition; all-consuming-yet-never-satisfied wants; a brutal temper; an impotence to love or be loved;

> divided homes and divided lives; small-minded and lop-
> sided pursuits; the vicious habit of depersonalizing
> everyone into a rival; uncontrolled and uncontrollable
> addictions; ugly parodies of community. I could go on.
> (Gal. 5:19–21 MSG)

All of these behavioral patterns sprout from the same seed—the flesh. We cannot console ourselves by saying that we have one sin, but not another. The flesh is a tree with different kinds of branches bearing many kinds of fruit, but all the fruit is sin. In me, it might produce outbursts of anger; in you, it might express itself in selfishness or pride. But both of us, though diverse in behavior and temperament, are controlled by the flesh. That's why self-righteousness, which always involves a spirit of compari-son, is so abhorrent to God. It thrives on a superficial view of sin ("mine is not as bad as yours") and an equally superficial view of God ("surely I'm within reach of His standards").

The Bible puts an end to such vanity. All have sinned, all by nature fulfill the desires of the flesh and of the mind (Rom. 3:23). We may think our sin is minor, but it needs the same drastic treatment as that of a criminal whose whole life has been twisted by perverse behavior. Our flesh and his are essentially the same—he may not have had our advantages, or perhaps God's grace has restrained us. In either case, pride is sinful.

If this sounds discouraging to those of us who think our sinful habit is of little importance, it ought to be *en*couraging to those of us who see ourselves as beyond hope. Our sinful pattern is no different in principle from that of other people. Some habits are more ingrained than others, but God's remedy for each is much the same.

The flesh, or the self, is so much a part of our thinking that we often do not even recognize its presence. Just in case you still think that you may have escaped its influence, here are some questions to ask yourself, based on a little tract called The Traits of the Self-Life.

Are you ever conscious of:

A secret spirit of pride; an exalted feeling in view of your success or position, because of your good training and appearance, because of your natural gifts and abilities; an important independent spirit; stiffness and preciseness?

Love of human praise, a secret fondness to be noticed; love of supremacy, drawing attention to self in conversation; a swelling out of self when you have had a free time in speaking or praying?

The stirrings of anger or impatience, which, worst of all, you call nervousness or holy indignation; a touchy, sensitive spirit; a disposition that dislikes being contradicted; a desire to throw sharp, heated words at another?

Self-will; a stubborn, unteachable spirit; an arguing, talkative spirit; harsh, sarcastic expressions; an unyielding, headstrong disposition; a driving, commanding spirit; a disposition to criticize and pick flaws when set aside and unnoticed; a peevish, fretful spirit; a disposition that loves to be coaxed and humored?

Carnal fear; a man-fearing spirit; a shrinking from reproach and duty; reasoning around your cross; a shrinking from doing your whole duty by those of wealth or position; a fearfulness that someone will offend and drive some prominent person away; a compromising spirit?

A jealous disposition; a secret spirit of envy shut up in your heart; an unpleasant sensation in view of the great prosperity and success of another; a disposition to speak of the faults and failings rather than the gifts and virtues of those more talented and appreciated than yourself?

A dishonest, deceitful disposition; the evading and covering of the truth; the covering up of your real faults; the leaving of a better impression of yourself than is strictly true; false humility; exaggeration, straining the truth?

Unbelief; a spirit of discouragement in times of pressure and opposition;

lack of quietness and confidence in God; lack of faith and trust in God; a disposition to worry and complain in the midst of pain, poverty, or at the dispensations of divine providence; an overanxious feeling about whether everything will come out all right?

Formality and deadness, lack of concern for lost souls; dryness and indifference; lack of power with God?

GOD'S SOLUTION

Fortunately, God chose to become involved in our predicament. The death of His Son was a solution designed to free us from the frustration of the self-driven life. We momentarily enjoy the works of the flesh, but later hate ourselves for what we have done. We resolve to change, yet later crave the same old sins.

Jesus' death accomplished many objectives. The cross is the basis for our forgiveness. It is also the basis for our spiritual freedom—deliverance from our stubborn habits. To appreciate what Christ did, we should become acquainted with two expressions: "in Adam" and "in Christ."

When Adam sinned, the whole human race was plunged into chaos. His descendants have never recovered from the debacle. Our sin nature was inherited from our parents, grandparents, and great grandparents; our ancestry can be traced back to the garden of Eden.

Just as a child might be born to a family that is in debt (and therefore the child inherits that debt), so we inherit the sinful nature of our forefather, Adam. And when our sin nature is left to itself, it causes us to react in unhealthy ways.

But because of Christ's death, believers are transferred from being "in Adam" to being "in Christ." God breaks our past ties, and Christ becomes our new ancestor. That's why Paul refers more than a hundred times to believers as being "in Christ." It's the basis for a whole new life.

All of this seems rather theoretical. Is there some value to this transfer of relationship? After all, when we were converted, we still looked the same, felt the same, and (unfortunately) often acted the same. On the surface, it sounds like being "in Christ" or "in Adam" is only a matter of words.

Not so. Think of a child who is adopted from one family into another. The fact of adoption doesn't change his appearance or his actions. But if he is taken from a family of slaves and adopted into a family of kings, he inherits a new set of relationships. There are new privileges and new responsibilities. That's why Paul could write, "Anyone united with the Messiah gets a fresh start, is created new. The old life is gone; a new life burgeons!" (2 Cor. 5:17 MSG).

Here's what happens: God identifies all believers with Christ, not in some mystical or theoretical way, but by changing our legal relationships. Before our conversion, we were obligated to obey the sinful impulses of our fallen nature. Even when we became tired of sin and resolved to change, the most we could do was rearrange our lives, but we could not change on the inside.

God has done what we could not do. He has given us a new nature, and the personal presence and power of the Holy Spirit so we can say no to our old nature.

To picture what God has done, think of yourself as a tenant in an apartment house. The landlord makes your life miserable and charges exorbitant rent. He mistreats you, barges into your apartment, wrecks the furniture, and then blames you for it. One day a new owner buys the apartment complex. You now have a kind landlord who invites you to live in the apartment for free. Not only that, but he fixes all of your furniture as well! You are relieved, grateful, and looking forward to a peaceful future.

A few hours later there is a knock on the door. To your amazement, there is your old landlord, looking as mean and demanding as ever. He threatens you, reminding you that you have rented from him for many years and are obligated to pay him and accept his authority.

What will you do? To resist him on your own is useless—he's more powerful than you are. Your best approach is to remind him you are now under a different management, so he'll have to take up your case with the new landlord.

How much obligation do you have to your old landlord? Your former landlord has no more right to demand a payment from you than he does from those whose names appear in the obituary column. That's why Paul exhorts us, "From now on, think of it this way: Sin speaks a dead language that means nothing to you; God speaks your mother tongue, and you hang on every word. You are dead to sin and alive to God" (Rom. 6:11 MSG). Your authority to say no to sin is God-given. Although before our conversion we were duty-bound to serve our inherited sin nature, this does not mean that everything we did was evil. Most people are able to control their desires and are capable of compassion and decency.

What it does mean is that we were never free from the futility of unsatisfied desires and frustrated passions. Pride, covetousness, and sensuality were our motivational drives. As believers purchased by God at the cost of His Son, our allegiance is now to Him. By the Holy Spirit He has given us the power to say no to our old sin nature and yes to a new life "in Christ."

WHERE THE RUBBER MEETS THE ROAD

How do you apply this knowledge when you want to break a specific habit? First, you must clearly see that in Christ you are already legally dead to your sinful passions. This is a point many people resist. They think, "I've got to become dead. I've got to pray that God will crucify me so that I will be alive in Christ." But that is precisely where they go wrong. Being dead to sin is not something that God promises you; it is not an act you beg Him to do. He simply declares it as a fact—already accomplished. Your failures and sins cannot change what God has said. Just because you get talked into obeying your old landlord doesn't change the fact of new management. All it means is that you forgot you could confidently say no to his extortion.

Let's say, for example, that you are a believer who lives with fear—perhaps a fear of people, disease, or loneliness. Then recognize those fears as a bill from your old landlord. Remember that you do not have to listen to him—much less do what he suggests. Take the matter up with your new manager. You are no longer duty-bound to those former relationships.

Second, you must admit the need for faith in your daily life. Your identification with Christ is not something that can be proved empirically. It's not like being able to see with our own eyes that the sun is shining. And even if it could be proven by our experience, many of us would be in trouble. An honest look at our lives hardly supports the idea that we are dead to sin and alive to God. But once we understand, with the Holy Spirit's help, that our ties with sin have already been broken, we begin to see that God has not deceived us. When we shift our attention to the completed work of the cross and insist on our privileges, our old self surrenders to God's authority. Through faith and faith alone we personalize our victory.

Let me add that freedom from sin is never automatic. Every inch is contested. No one ever falls into maturity, even though we are already positionally complete in Christ. One danger of reading a book like this is that we may tend to look for formulas for a new spiritual technique. But there is no substitute for waiting before God, reading His Word, and then obeying the truth He has revealed.

The Christian life is a growing relationship. Applying the cross to your life is not something you do once. Nor is it sufficient to do it every week or even once a day. It is a moment by moment, daily process. As you develop sensitivity to the Holy Spirit's work in your life, you will find that saying no to the flesh and yes to Christ will become a way of life. In the next chapter, you will learn how to personalize Christ's victory.

QUESTIONS FOR GROUP STUDY
OR PERSONAL REFLECTION

1. If you have not already done so, now is the time to take stock of your life, asking what behavior patterns or thoughts you must allow God to begin to change.

2. Read Romans 6—8, carefully underlining each instance in which Paul uses the expression "free from sin" or its equivalent. In each case, find what Paul gives as a basis for your freedom.

3. The more clearly you see the wide-ranging benefits of the cross, the more you will develop a life of habitual praise. Begin this habit by thanking God three times a day for the victory Christ accomplished on your behalf.

4. Begin each day by giving it to God. Take time to:
   a. Give thanks that Christ has already conquered the problems you will face that day.
   b. Accept by faith the victory Christ won at the cross—before you are tempted to sin.

Chapter 6

THE POWER OF THE HOLY SPIRIT

Years ago when slavery was officially abolished in Jamaica, some of the slaves in the remote areas did not know of their freedom. Years after their release had been announced they still continued to serve their masters, oblivious to the fact that they were legally free. Their owners kept the news from the slaves as long as possible, hoping to extract every ounce of work from their captives. The slaves wouldn't have had to put up with their drudgery—except for their ignorance of the facts.

Jesus Christ issues a proclamation of liberty to every believer. We've already learned that our union with Him qualifies us to share His victory. But precisely how is His victory translated into our experience? The answer lies in the personal ministry of the Holy Spirit. He communicates Christ's strength to us. He satisfies our spiritual thirst. Let's consider what Jesus had to say about the Spirit's ministry.

When Jesus attended the Feast of Tabernacles at Jerusalem, He was deeply moved by the emptiness of the ritual the Jews dutifully performed. Bible scholars tell us that on that day, a group of white-robed priests went down to the pool of Siloam. They filled their jars with water from the pool and then walked home to the temple and poured out the water in the presence of the people. This symbolic act was to remind them of how God had supplied the Israelites' need for water during their wandering in the wilderness.

This ceremony was a beautiful reminder of what God had done, but the people missed its spiritual meaning—that God wanted to satisfy their spiritual thirst as well. The Scripture says: "On the final and climactic day of the Feast, Jesus took his stand. He cried out, 'If anyone thirsts, let him come to me and drink. Rivers of living water will brim and spill out of the depths of anyone who believes in me this way, just as the Scripture says.' (He said this in regard to the Spirit, whom those who believed in him were about to receive. The Spirit had not yet been given because Jesus had not yet been glorified)" (John 7:37–39 MSG). Jesus was predicting the coming of the new age when the Holy Spirit would be poured out upon His people.

Notice carefully that the basis of the gift of the Spirit is the glorification of Jesus Christ. The Spirit, Jesus said, could not be given to His people until He was glorified. God doesn't give the Spirit to His people because they agonize for Him or fast. Rather, the Spirit is given because Jesus has ascended into heaven. In the Old Testament era, the Spirit's work was limited; after Christ's ascension, the Spirit was given to every believer.

Listen to the words of Jesus to His followers: "Let me say it again, this truth: It's better for you that I leave. If I don't leave, the Friend won't come. But if I go, I'll send him to you" (John 16:7 MSG). Jesus could not give the Spirit to the church until He left this earth physically. He had to be glorified before the Spirit could descend upon His people.

Think of it this way. Jesus Christ's death on the cross is the basis for our forgiveness. Because He took our penalty, we can receive forgiveness of sins without strings attached; the only requirement is trust—a transfer of our faith from ourselves to Jesus alone. Similarly, the basis on which the Holy Spirit is given is Jesus' ascension and glorification. We don't have to beg for forgiveness, nor do we need to agonize for the Spirit; the Water of Life is also free, and is received by faith.

Ever since Christ was glorified, and the Spirit was given on the day of Pentecost, every believer has received Him (Rom. 8:9; 1 Cor. 6:19). There is no need for striving, anxiety, or a feeling that we are unworthy to receive Him. He is waiting to quench our thirst, but His control in our lives is never automatic.

HOW DO WE RECEIVE THE SPIRIT'S POWER?

Do you know the reaction of many Christians when someone talks to them about walking in the fullness of the Holy Spirit? They say, "That's great for others, but I'm not good enough. I don't qualify. If I were more dedicated and spent more time in Bible reading and prayer, I might eventually be worthy to walk in the Spirit."

But they've got it backward. The Holy Spirit is not given to those who have it all together spiritually; He is given to enable them to get it together spiritually! I'm struck with Paul's words: "My counsel is this: Live freely, animated and motivated by God's Spirit. Then you won't feed the compulsions of selfishness" (Gal. 5:16 MSG). Notice the sequence. Paul does not say that if we stop carrying out the desires of the flesh we will walk in the Spirit; rather, he says that if we walk in the Spirit, we will not fulfill the desires of the flesh!

The order makes an incredible difference. Christians often ignore any thought of walking by the Spirit, because they think they are not good enough. Their life is too filled with fleshly struggles. But that's like refusing to accept medicine until we get well and feel worthy of it! The whole purpose of medicine is to enable us to get well. It is given to the sick, not the healthy. In the same way, the Spirit is given to enable us to break sin's power; we don't have to do that on our own before we receive the Spirit's power.

Imagine someone saying, "I'm not good enough to be saved; I'm going to wait until I get myself together before I come to Christ." We would quickly point out that salvation is designed for sinners. None of us is ever good enough to be saved; we are saved because of God's great generosity in Jesus Christ. People who say they aren't good enough are missing the point of Jesus' death.

But the same applies to the Holy Spirit. As Jesus' death gives us forgiveness, so Jesus' ascension and glorification give us the Holy Spirit. And the coming of the Holy Spirit into our lives is not just a window dressing. He indwells us so that we might allow Him to control us.

I believe that we have often made the requirements for walking in the Spirit too complicated. We've stressed dedication, surrender, and discipline as prerequisites to receiving and walking in the power of the Holy Spirit. When I read books that give seven steps to the filling of the Spirit or others that condense it to four, I find myself asking, "Can any one of us be sure we have fully carried out all of these requirements?" Is not the Spirit's power given to sinners to enable them to be yielded and disciplined, rather than expecting all of these characteristics from them first?

Notice Jesus' words: "If anyone thirsts, let him come to me and drink" (John 7:37 MSG). The only requirement is a thirst that will draw us to come to Him. We don't have to be supersaints, just thirsty sinners. That's why Jesus could offer living water to a woman who had had five husbands and was living in a common-law marriage. He promised that from within her would burst forth living water that would quench her emotional and spiritual thirst (John 4:10–14).

Are you thirsty? Do you feel, as I have often felt, like an apple tree trying to grow in a desert? Then you are a candidate for the Spirit's life and power.

LIFE IN THE SPIRIT

There is a direct connection between walking in the Spirit and breaking a sinful habit. Today, many people suffer from drug addiction. Perhaps they began getting high just for kicks, or because they wanted to look cool, but now they are hooked. Drugs as we know them today were not available in New Testament times, but many people were addicted to wine, which led Paul to write to the believers in Ephesus, "Don't drink too much wine. That cheapens your life. Drink the Spirit of God, huge draughts of him" (Eph. 5:18 MSG). To those who are struggling with addiction of any kind, the Bible offers a different master: Be controlled by the Spirit, rather than drugs or alcohol or any other stubborn habit. The Spirit's control will replace sin's control. His power is greater than the power of all your sin put together.

Perhaps you're wondering at this point, "OK, how do I get hold of this power?" You begin by clearing the deck. Confess your sin—and the sin must be confessed—and receive God's forgiveness. Claim 1 John 1:9, "If we confess our sins, He is faithful and righteous to forgive us our sins and to cleanse us from all unrighteousness."

Then remember that the Holy Spirit desires to energize you. Don't ever think that He is reluctant, waiting to be coaxed into the driver's seat of your life. He became a resident with the express purpose of becoming president. But He will not exercise His power apart from your faith. If you ask Him to control you, believe that He will.

Maybe you feel unworthy, or perhaps you think that there will be a more convenient time. F. B. Meyer tells of his experience: "I left the prayer meeting and crept away into the lane praying, 'O Lord, if there was ever a man who needs the power of the Holy Spirit, it is I. But I do not know how to receive Him. I am too tired, too worn, too nervously run down to agonize.' Then a voice said to me, 'As you took forgiveness from the hand of the dying Christ, take the Holy Spirit from the hand of the living Christ.'" Meyer goes on to say, "I took for the first time and have kept on taking ever since."

How were you saved? By depending on the *death* of Jesus Christ. How do you receive the power of the Spirit? By depending on the *ascension* of

Jesus Christ. Both come by faith. That's why Paul wrote, "My counsel for you is simple and straightforward: Just go ahead with what you've been given. You received Christ Jesus, the Master; now live him. You're deeply rooted in him. You're well constructed upon him. You know your way around the faith. Now do what you've been taught" (Col. 2:6 MSG).

You receive the Spirit's filling by faith, not by having a particular feeling. Some Christians wrongly believe that the filling of the Spirit is a sensation. They expect waves of love, an overwhelming sense of peace, or the ability to speak in strange languages. Theirs is a fleshly desire to walk by sight, not by faith. We find it difficult to take God at His Word, and like the Pharisees, we ask for a sign that we might believe.

God, however, delights when we believe in Him without demanding emotional crutches. Just as a new believer needs to receive God's promises—apart from feelings—so we daily need to receive the power of the Holy Spirit—apart from feelings.

LIVING BY PRAISE

You will be greatly helped in accepting the Spirit's control if you learn the power of praise. "It's the praising life that honors me. As soon as you set your foot on the Way, I'll show you my salvation" (Ps. 50:23 MSG). Paul put it this way: "Be cheerful no matter what; pray all the time; thank God no matter what happens. This is the way God wants you who belong to Christ Jesus to live" (1 Thess. 5:18 MSG).

When we read these exhortations to praise, we tend to make two very common errors. One is to think we should praise God only for the good things He gives us—health, food, clothes, and other blessings. The second is to think that we should praise God only when we feel like doing so. But Paul wrote, "In everything give thanks." That means in all circumstances, whether pleasant or painful.

I find it extremely difficult to give thanks to God when my personal relationships run amuck and everything else that really matters also goes wrong. But it's only when we choose to give praise in the rough spots of life that we begin to see them from God's perspective. Furthermore, if we don't give thanks in all things, we are living in unbelief, for we are assuming that our circumstances are not controlled by a God who loves us. I'm not saying that you should give thanks for sin, but you can thank God for how He will use that sin to teach, to rebuke, or to humble you.

Also, you can learn to give thanks even if you don't feel particularly thankful. If God gives a command, He expects obedience, whether you are in the mood or not. Thankfulness, like forgiveness, is not an emotion. Thankfulness is an intelligent response of gratitude to God, based on His Word. It is your determination to be obedient.

Here's what to do: Name your sin, and give thanks to God that in Jesus you already are victorious over it. When Jesus died on the cross, He provided forgiveness and freedom. Thank God for both, saying something like: "Father, I thank You that I am in Christ. I thank You that my position is secure and immovable. I thank You that in Him I've already won the victory over the sin that besets me. And I thank You that I am free." Soon your experience will catch up with what God has already given you in Christ.

I'm not talking about a once-and-for-all act of thanksgiving. David wrote, "I bless God every chance I get; my lungs expand with his praise" (Ps. 34:1 MSG). But how does praise become a way of life, a daily habit, more regular than tying your shoes or combing your hair?

You don't learn to praise in a day, especially since you may have been complaining for years! New habits take time to develop. But you can begin today, and practice tomorrow, and the next day, until it becomes part of you. "Let the Word of Christ—the Message—have the run of the house. Give it plenty of room in your lives. Instruct and direct one another using good common sense. And sing, sing your hearts out to God!" (Col. 3:16 MSG).

The Holy Spirit is willing. Are you?

QUESTIONS FOR GROUP STUDY
OR PERSONAL REFLECTION

1. Paul lists nine fruits of the Spirit (Gal. 5:22–23). Which two are the most evident in your life? Which two are the least evident? Take some time now to ask God to help you improve in the areas in which you are lacking.

2. Think specifically of ways in which the fruit of the Spirit can be further developed. These questions might help:
   a. What obstacles in your life hinder the ministry of the Spirit? Unconfessed sin? Strained personal relationships? Lack of commitment? Little or no time spent in Bible reading or prayer?
   b. Have you ever asked God to control you with His Spirit? Remember, we often have not because we ask not (James 4:2). Why not simply thank Him for His control each day, knowing that He will give you strength?

3. The most important ingredient in releasing the Spirit's power in our lives is faith. Our faith is strengthened by (a) making the Word of God the focus of our attention, and (b) developing the habit of praise. Write down some creative ways to make these practices a part of your daily activity.

4. Regardless of your current life circumstances, spend some time in
   prayer right now thanking God for who He is and what He has done
   for you. Ask Him to increase the "thankfulness" aspect of your daily
   prayer life.

Chapter 7

THE RENEWING OF YOUR MIND

Have you given your anxiety to God only to find an hour later that the weight is back on your shoulders? Do you ask God to control your temper, but still blow your top? Have you prayed not to lust, or even reckoned yourself dead to sinful impulses, only to find that tall blonde from the coffee shop walking around in your mind again the next morning?

We surrender ourselves to God, but so soon and so easily revert to our old habits. We mean well, yet fare so poorly. Why?

Jesus told a story that illustrates the most important single principle in breaking a sinful habit. There once was a man who had been inhabited by a demon. The demon caused the man to do awful things and controlled every area of his life, but one day the demon was expelled and the man danced with joy. The evil spirit then passed through waterless places, seeking rest. Finding none, it decided to return to its original house, right in the center of the poor man's life. To its satisfaction, the demon saw that its original living space was unoccupied. It then found seven other spirits even more evil than itself to go and live there with it. Sadly, the man, who just a short time earlier had been dancing with joy, was now worse off than he was when he started (Luke 11:24–26).

Why did this man fail in his quest for freedom? He didn't understand the principle of replacement. None of us can overcome evil by simply renouncing it. Rather, we can only do so by substituting good in its place. Sinful habits cannot be broken without replacing them with righteous ones.

Try this simple experiment. Think of the number eight. Have you visualized it? If so, exercise your willpower and stop thinking of the number eight right now.

Were you able to do it? Of course not. At least, I'm still thinking about that number. Can we, by sheer willpower, stop thinking about the number eight? By no means. Trying to push it out of our minds actually causes us to focus our attention on it.

What a picture of us when we try to overcome sin. We may get on our knees and ask God to take the desire away; we then determine not to think those lurid or greedy thoughts, but there they are again. We resist them once more, trying desperately to push them out of our minds. But we are trapped. Try as we might, we just can't get them to budge.

Can we really be free? Yes, we can control those thoughts, but not by trying to stop thinking about them! To simply resist evil is to make it grow stronger. Our determination not to think lustful thoughts only reinforces them in our thought patterns.

How, then, can we be free? Let's return to our experiment once more and think of the number eight. Although we can't stop thinking about it by sheer resistance, we can push that number out of our minds quite easily. Here's how: Think about one or two bits of information about your mother. Reminisce about your place in the family, whether you are still connected with it or disconnected. Concentrate on this new information, and you'll stop thinking of the number eight.

You can handle sinful thought patterns in the same way. Fear, lust, covetousness—all of these can be squeezed out of your mind by turning your thoughts to the Scriptures. Freedom comes by filling your mind with God's thoughts (Rom. 12:1–2; Phil. 4:8).

I know a young man whose wife died of cancer. She suffered intensely during the last weeks of her life. Yet she and her husband were able to accept this tragedy without bitterness or the slightest trace of self-pity. I asked John, "Why were you and your wife able to accept this so well? Weren't you ever resentful and angry at God through this ordeal?" His reply: "Yes, we had moments like that. But when they came, I read the Scriptures to my wife. Then we bought the whole New Testament on CD, and we played it in our house, hour after hour." That was the secret—expelling angry and anxious thoughts by filling the mind with the Word of God.

What is the best way to take air out of a bottle? Possibly someone could suggest that we build an elaborate vacuum pump to suck out the air. But there is a simpler solution. If we fill the bottle with water, the air has to leave.

To diffuse the power of sin, you need to have your thought patterns replaced by the Word of God. Every temptation, vice, or sinister motive comes to you by your thoughts; these must be brought under the control of the Holy Spirit. Paul wrote, "Don't become so well-adjusted to your culture that you fit into it without even thinking. Instead, fix your attention on God. You'll be changed from the inside out" (Rom. 12:2 MSG). The difference between worldliness and godliness is a renewed mind. This old adage puts it straight: You aren't what you think you are; but what you *think*, you are!

Let us suppose we could flash all the thoughts we had last week on a giant screen—not a one of us would like to have others view the details! Yet, discouraging though this would be, *that* is who we really are! Our thoughts not only shape our life; they *are* our life.

Somewhere I read about a man recently released from prison who was having difficulty adjusting to his freedom. He tried this experiment: He took a glass bottle with a distinct shape and crammed it full of wires, some small and some large. After some time had passed he smashed the bottle with a hammer. The result? Most of the wires retained the shape of the bottle. Those wires had to be straightened out, one by one.

That man discovered that it is possible to be technically free and still retain the traits of bondage. Even though a person is liberated, he or she must adjust to freedom and carefully dismantle the habits of the past.

As a believer, you are legally free in Christ, but you can still be enslaved by the fantasies of the flesh and the vices of the world. You can yield, surrender, and pray, but your mind will revert to familiar territory as soon as your experience wears thin. To break this self-defeating cycle, you need to outline a specific strategy for experiencing the freedom you have in Christ and accept the victory that is legally yours.

PREPARE FOR BATTLE

Is this really possible? Yes. But not without locking horns with wicked spiritual forces. Read carefully Paul's words: "The world doesn't fight fair. But we don't live or fight our battles that way—never have and never will. The tools of our trade aren't for marketing or manipulation, but they are for demolishing that entire massively corrupt culture. We use our powerful God-tools for smashing warped philosophies, tearing down barriers erected against the truth of God, fitting every loose thought and emotion and impulse into the structure of life shaped by Christ" (2 Cor. 10:3–5 MSG).

You have the spiritual artillery needed to destroy the fortresses of the mind. Vain reasoning, powerful imaginations, and perverted attitudes can be routed. You have the spiritual equipment to track down thoughts and make them captive to Christ.

Military moves are made according to determined strategy. Weapons need to be understood before they are used. In this battle with Satan and evil, you need to know the strategy, and be well acquainted with your weapons. But, specifically, how can you do this?

First, you must identify the alien thoughts that you want to replace. You must name the fantasies, imaginations, and attitudes that you want to be rid of. To say, "I want to be a better Christian" or "I want to be more joyful" will not do. Generalities are no good. You must be specific.

I assume that you know the sins in your life that won't budge. In fact, if you have participated in all the questions in this book to this point, you should already have a very good idea of your chief struggles. Now, take a sheet of paper and jot down which thought patterns have to go. Don't skip this step! Few people actually write down their goals, and fewer still actually accomplish what they haven't written down, so it is very important to write down the parts of your life that you want to change.

Second, be prepared for the discipline of spiritual warfare. The world, the flesh, and the devil do not surrender without a struggle. If you want to be blessed by God, you must learn to "chew on Scripture day and night" (Ps. 1:2 MSG).

Sometimes we are told, "We are in a spiritual battle. As soldiers of the cross we must be disciplined; we must put effort and sacrifice into the Christian life." Then perhaps a week later, another Christian appears to say the opposite. "I was working too hard at being a Christian; God showed me that I had to just relax—*rest* in the Lord."

Though these viewpoints appear contradictory, they really are not. *Only a Christian who is disciplined in the Word of God can rest in the Lord.* Yes, we can cease our striving and learn to relax in the confidence that God is equal to every situation. But a lazy, undisciplined Christian cannot do so; he falls apart at the seams when tragedy strikes. The believer who is "like a tree planted by the rivers of water" (Ps. 1:3 KJV) is the one who meditates in the law of God every free moment (v. 2); his thoughts turn to the Word of God like steel to a magnet.

Declaring war on your thought life means that you must set aside time every morning to begin your offensive attack. I suggest twenty minutes as a minimum. Meditation in the Scriptures requires effort; nothing worth having can be achieved without exertion.

You've heard the cliche "a chapter a day keeps the devil away." Don't you believe it. You can read a chapter of the Bible with your mind on tomorrow's business deal or with a heart full of revenge. Real meditation requires quality time. You must assimilate a passage and give it your unhurried attention.

Finally, be prepared to memorize the Word of God. "I've banked your promises in the vault of my heart so I won't sin myself bankrupt" (Ps. 119:11 MSG). Rather than memorizing verses at random, take your list of troublesome thought patterns and find verses of Scripture that speak directly to them. Specific examples are given at the end of this chapter. Memorize these verses so that you have them at your fingertips during the day—you'll need them. The only alternative to memorizing verses is typing them out on small note cards so that you can have them for immediate reference. These are the passages that God will use to demolish the present strongholds of your mind and construct a new edifice.

USE YOUR ARTILLERY

So far you've identified your sins, you've decided to set aside twenty minutes for God each morning, and you've even gotten some passages of Scripture to work with. Now what? What should you do tomorrow morning? Your strategy should begin the moment you awake. Those moments between waking up and getting your feet on the floor are crucial. The seeds of discouragement, anger, and lust begin there. While still in bed, thank God for the rest He has given you. I personally pray, "Today I get up in the name of the Father, the Son, and the Holy Spirit." Consciously commit your mind, opportunities, and time to Him. Remind yourself of God's promises. Here are a few:

Nothing, you see, is impossible with God. (Luke 1:37 MSG)

And we know that God causes all things to work together
for good to those who love God, to those who are called
according to His purpose. (Rom. 8:28)

I can do all things through Him who strengthens me.
(Phil. 4:13)

Reminding yourself of God's promises gives you the proper perspective on life.

Then after you're out of bed and reasonably awake (I need coffee—lots of coffee—to get my mind in gear), read a chapter from the Bible, observing what God is saying to you.

Then spend some time to prepare your mind for the particular temptation you will face that day. Let's suppose your boss habitually irritates you. An hour after you arrive at work, you wish you could scream. If you wait until your boss shouts at you before you decide how you will respond, you'll probably react in anger. Use the Word of God in anticipation. During your time with God in the morning, recite the verses you have memorized and claim Christ's victory before your boss blows his fuse.

The same principle applies whether you're struggling with an eating disorder, pornography, tobacco, or alcohol. Claim God's promises for that particular day. Tell Him that with His help you resolve to choose Him rather than the world.

But remember, if you wait until temptation arrives to decide how you will react, you've waited too long! Choose beforehand to claim God's promises for whatever circumstances you expect to encounter.

Then, during the day, learn to obey the first promptings of the Holy

Spirit. If you are tempted to enjoy a sensual fantasy, deal with those thoughts immediately. Each of us knows when we let our minds skip across that invisible line into forbidden territory. The moment we do so, we sense we are violating the purity the Holy Spirit desires. That is the moment to say, "I reject these thoughts in the name of Jesus." And then quote the passages of Scripture you have learned for that temptation. With time, your sensitivity to the Holy Spirit will develop.

Most important, learn to switch topics on the flesh and the Devil. Remember the experiment at the beginning of this chapter? We couldn't stop thinking of the number eight, no matter how hard we tried. Only switching to another topic could produce this result.

You can do this with any temptation you face. Simply use your temptation as an alarm system—a signal to give praise to God. If, for example, you fear cancer (since one out of four people in the United States will have the disease, your fears may have a statistical basis), use that fear as an opportunity to give glory to God. Quote Romans 8:35–39 or read Psalms 103, 144, or 145. Then thank God for all the blessings you have in Christ. Thank Him for forgiveness, for His sovereignty, power, and love. In this way, your stumbling block will be changed into a stepping-stone. You'll be praising rather than pouting.

While I was writing this chapter, a woman called on the phone to ask me to pray that she would overcome her battle with smoking. She had tried to be free, but hadn't succeeded. I gave her several suggestions; one was to accept the desire for a cigarette as a reminder that it was time to read three chapters of praise to God. Rather than concentrating on the desire, she could focus on God and His power. Eventually, she would learn that she did not have to yield to this temptation; the very struggle would become God's way of building discipline into her life. Unfortunately, the more I probed, the more I realized there was a whole cluster of other issues in her life that vied for resolution. As mentioned in a previous chapter, it is difficult to tackle one destructive habit while planning to tolerate other such habits at the same time. God intends to change the core of our motivations and values.

If your problem is unhealthy eating—whether you eat too much or too little—decide that your urges will be a reminder to divert your attention to God's Word. Memorize a verse of Scripture, pray for your missionary friends, sing a hymn of praise. By outlining and following a specific strategy to resist temptation, you will eventually be free from its grip.

Finally, do not be discouraged by the frequency of the same temptation. If you have lived a long time with sinful thought patterns, the strongholds of your imagination will not be easily toppled. Furthermore, you must recognize the possibility that you are not merely confronting yourself, but satanic forces as well. Satan's most used weapon is discouragement. After you have rejected insidious thoughts, he delights in having them pop back into your mind. Since his activity has become so overt in our society, a later chapter will give specific instruction on how to confront these forces. Let me say in advance that the most important insulation you have against satanic attack is personal righteousness—confessing and forsaking sin. And as you apply the above principles consistently, Satan and his forces will be weakened. Eventually they will flee.

How long does it take for the mind to be renewed? That depends. Some Christians who apply these principles recognize a noticeable difference within a week. Others who are steeped in decades of sin may need months before they can say, "I am free!" And, of course, no one reaches perfection. The more we meditate on the Word, the more clearly we see new areas of our lives that need to be changed. Subtle motives often surface only after long exposure to the light of God's Word.

I once counseled a man who struggled with homosexual temptations but was freed from his former way of life by using the above suggestions. He confessed that he often used to lapse back into his former thought patterns. "But now," he says, "when I think the thoughts I used to think, I get sick to my stomach." He is proof of what God can do in the life of anyone who persistently meditates in His Word and applies it directly to areas of spiritual conflict.

I'm convinced that God intends us to be free from mental bondage. His Word is the resource by which our thoughts can become obedient to Him. Even Christ, the eternal Son of God, "learned obedience from the things which He suffered" (Heb. 5:8). And if He, the Son, sets you free, you will be free indeed (John 8:36).

QUESTIONS FOR GROUP STUDY
OR PERSONAL REFLECTION

The following Scripture references can be used to begin the process of bringing your thoughts under the control of the Holy Spirit. Additional passages can be found through careful reading of the Scriptures along with the use of a concordance or Nave's Topical Bible.

Covetousness
Psalm 119:36; Luke 12:15; Colossians 3:1–2, 5–6; Philippians 4:11–12; 1 Timothy 6:6; Hebrews 13:5

Pride
Proverbs 16:18; Galatians 6:3, 14; James 4:6; 1 Peter 5:5–6

Lack of discipline
Romans 12:11; 1 Corinthians 9:26–27; Philippians 4:12—13; Hebrews 6:12

Lust
Romans 6:11–12; 2 Corinthians 10:4–5; Ephesians 4:22–24; Philippians 4:8; 1 Peter 2:11

Anger
Psalm 37:8; Proverbs 14:29; 16:32; Ephesians 4:26, 31; Colossians 3:8; James 1:19–20

Worry
Matthew 6:25–34; Philippians 4:6; 1 Peter 5:7

Bitterness
Ephesians 4:31–32; Hebrews 12:15

Unhealthy Eating
Judges 3:14–22; Proverbs 23:20–21; 1 Corinthians 9:27; 10:31–33; Philippians 4:12

1. How much time do you really spend in God's Word on a daily basis? Be honest! Admitting your need in that area of your life is the first step toward positive growth. Now spend some time in prayer and ask God to increase your desire to meditate on the Scriptures daily.

2. Earlier in the chapter we talked about replacing one set of thoughts with another. What are some things you can think about as a means of overcoming temptation? Which Scriptures should you memorize so you can think of them clearly during times of temptation? Is there anyone you can call, day or night, when temptation begins to overcome you?

3. Spiritual warfare is real. Take some time right now to specifically name the areas in which you have been struggling. Pray that God would help you overcome these trials, and the blood of Christ would help you stand against the Evil One.

Chapter 8

LIVING WITH YOUR FEELINGS

Our generation places a high priority on feeling good. If you watch the ads on TV, you know how to reach this goal. First, you must surround yourself with the right things—the latest styles in clothing, an expensive new car, a home in the right neighborhood, just to start with. Second, you should look attractive; if necessary have plastic surgery so you can turn heads in any room. Finally, you should not worry how your actions will affect those around you. "If it feels good, do it!"

It is significant that the first sin ever committed was caused by someone choosing to follow personal feelings instead of God's commands. The fruit of this tree, Eve was told, would satisfy her hunger in ways that the fruit of the other trees could not. She would gain wisdom and become queen of her own domain. Little did she know the consequences such a decision would carry. Ever since that time, humanity has been driven by feelings or desires even when they are not in harmony with God's commands. Of course, feelings in themselves are not evil. God created us with the ability to feel pain and joy; Jesus Himself is "touched with the feeling of our infirmities" (Heb. 4:15 KJV). To stoically ignore our feelings or reject them out of hand is to invite callousness and indifference. Paul condemned the wicked who were no longer capable of compassion, who were past feeling (Eph. 4:19). But our feelings are not a fully reliable guide for behavior. Many feelings must be restrained, both for our good and the good of others.

Our will must provide a check on the stream of emotions that ebb and flow through our being. If we follow our feelings wherever they lead, we will be fulfilling virtually every wanton desire. Of course, all of us have feelings that are a part of being human, but if these feelings rage out of control they can result either in anger or in depression, in which case special counseling may be necessary.

In this chapter we will discuss self-control and our need to submit our desires to God's lordship. When Jesus spoke to His tempter, He said, "Man shall not live on bread alone, but on every word that proceeds out of the mouth of God" (Matt. 4:4). He was suggesting the principle of balance, of a life under the authority of the revealed Word of God.

PITFALLS OF LIVING BY FEELING

Before I suggest how you can cope with your emotions, I want you to consider what happens when you live by the dictates of your own hunches and whims. A life based on desires is an invitation to the sin of disobedience. Often our feelings run counter to what God requires. In fact, most sinful habits are developed by simply following the path of least resistance, by doing whatever we feel like doing. Many of our struggles can be traced to sensuality, and by that I mean being controlled by our physical senses. This spawns defeat, self-absorption, and unbelief.

Many people who think they cannot obey God's commandments simply don't feel like obeying. Occasionally they have days when they wake up wanting to do what God requires—but not often. Our fallen human nature never feels like obeying God; usually it wants to do its own thing. This attitude comes from Satan as he suggests to us—as he did to Eve— that God has asked us to obey commands that we cannot or need not keep. If we think we can't obey God until we *feel* like it, we will never get off the ground in our spiritual lives.

Let's be specific. In his book on overcoming difficulties in marriage, Jay Adams writes of a particular counseling situation in which all love had been drained from the marriage and the partners had already agreed to a divorce. Neither one had committed a serious sin against the marriage. They just didn't *feel* in love anymore. They went to the counselor hoping he would confirm their decision that since there was no feeling left, they should divorce. The couple was shocked to find the counselor saying, "If you don't love each other, there is only one thing to do: You will have to *learn* to love one another." The couple was incredulous. "How can you learn to love someone? You can't produce feelings out of thin air!"

The counselor explained that in the Bible, God commands us to love one another. When the husband was told that he should love his wife as Christ loved the church, he gasped. He could never do that. But the counselor persisted. He explained that the husband should begin on a lesser level. The Bible also commands us to love our neighbor, and since his wife is his closest neighbor, he should love her. But even so, the husband rejected the idea that he could love his wife that way. Then the counselor explained that he was still not off the hook, for God had commanded us to love even our enemies!

This couple had made a common error; they had equated love with feelings. In the Bible, love is not a feeling. We can learn to love, even though we begin with little or no emotional impetus. In other words, we can choose to love. And God gives us the grace to do so.

Love is not an emotion; neither is forgiveness. The Bible commands us to put away all bitterness (Eph. 4:31); we are to forgive others whether they solicit our forgiveness or not (v. 32). Yet many Christians believe that they can't forgive until they feel like it! They think that if they forgive when they don't feel like it, they are hypocritical.

However, if forgiveness were an emotion, God would be commanding us to do the impossible. We cannot switch our emotions on and off. We cannot develop the right feelings on our own. But God is not mocking us when He tells us to forgive; we can choose to do so, whether we feel like it or not. Never try to skirt God's commands under the pretense that you don't feel like obeying Him.

A second danger of living by feelings is that you may tend to derive your doctrine from feelings. If you believe God is with you just because "He feels so close," you will also believe there are days when He forsakes you because "He feels so far away." The assurance of God's presence does not come by feelings, but by faith (Heb. 13:5). Fortunately, you don't always have to feel God's presence to be in fellowship with Him and to make spiritual progress.

The apostle Paul, who by any standard lived a successful, victorious Christian life, had his bad days. "We don't want you in the dark, friends, about how hard it was when all this came down on us in Asia province. It was so bad we didn't think we were going to make it. We felt like we'd been sent to death row, that it was all over for us" (2 Cor. 1:8 MSG). Have you ever been restless, unable to control your fluctuating emotions? Paul wrote that he had no rest in his spirit until Titus came to him with some good news from the church (2 Cor. 2:13).

Even more surprising is the testimony of Jesus. As He approached the cross, He was tempted to call a halt to the whole plan of redemption. He was deeply vexed in spirit. "Now My soul has become troubled; and what shall I say, 'Father, save Me from this hour'? But for this purpose I came to this hour. Father, glorify Your name'" (John 12:27–28).

Jesus' agony in Gethsemane is well documented, as His soul was troubled "to the point of death" (Matt. 26:38). Emotionally, He shrank from the pain and torture that lie ahead and asked if it were possible that the cup of suffering might pass from Him (v. 39). All these emotional upheavals took place in the God-man, the One who lived perfectly, sinlessly.

Now, it is often true that depression is the result of sin, particularly anger, self-pity, or unresolved guilt. For example, a woman who had seen half a dozen counselors could not cope with the intense periods of depression she faced. Despite hours of counsel, she had withheld one important bit of information, namely that as a teenage girl she had given birth to a baby and had killed it to avoid the stigma attached to her illicit sexual affair. But when she finally admitted her sin, confessed it, and accepted God's forgiveness, the depression left. Self-pity, hostility, and warped values can have the same effect. That is why those who think they have emotional problems often discover that their problems are not really emotional. Indeed, their emotions are working only too well. Their emotional struggles are often symptomatic of unresolved guilt from sin that they have been unwilling to face.

However, at times you may experience emotional turbulence that may not be related to any particular sin. The cause may be physiological, or perhaps Satan is trying to disrupt your fellowship with God. At any rate, this point needs emphasis: You do not need to experience a steady stream of placid emotional feelings to walk with God.

Emotions fluctuate. They are perhaps only a little more dependable than the weather. Today you feel great, tonight you can't sleep, and tomorrow life seems pointless. Those moments provide a crucial test of whether you have learned to walk by faith or whether you are still dependent on emotional sight. Personally, I'm glad that my acceptance before God is unrelated to the way I feel!

A third consequence of living by feelings is that you develop the sin of procrastination. It's time to visit a friend in the hospital, write a letter or e-mail, or do some chores at home. You know what you ought to do, but for some mysterious reason you can't seem to get started. You stall, putter around, watch TV. In short, you procrastinate. Why?

There may be several reasons. You may feel frustrated because the work seems overwhelming; or you may feel inferior, unable to do the job as well as someone else. So you sit around, waiting for the magic moment when suddenly everything will fall into place. But those magic moments never come, and your responsibilities never go away.

The result is that you begin to feel guilty for not doing what you know you should. Putting matters off does not relieve tension, but increases it. Perhaps the most tragic consequence of living according to feelings is that such a life ends up being self-defeating. It seems reasonable to believe that the sure path to happiness is to be able to do whatever you feel like doing. But if you follow that reasoning eventually you will realize that you aren't enjoying your feelings. Shrugging off responsibility only increases guilt. The more you give in to your feelings, the worse you feel. Rather than satisfying your feelings, you actually cause restlessness and dissatisfaction.

A man may be depressed because he is unable to finish his work around the house. He hopes that someday he will feel like taking out the garbage, trimming the hedges, washing the cars, and fixing the fence. But right now he doesn't feel like it. Furthermore, even if he began today, there would be more work tomorrow. So he follows his feelings and lies on the sofa, watching TV. Since he is doing what he feels like doing, he should be happy and satisfied, right?

Wrong! Guilt settles upon him like London fog. Each day the work he should be doing piles up higher and higher. His children and his spouse begin to complain. But he is so far behind, there is no use trying to catch up. His frustration will never leave until he chooses to do what he ought, whether he feels like it or not.

The moment you declare war on your besetting sin, you will bump into your feelings, mostly unhelpful ones. Be prepared for a feeling of helplessness, the feeling that you are the victim of circumstances you cannot change and desires you cannot control. These feelings just happen to be the sin of unbelief in a different form. They are one of the tools Satan uses to get you to believe that either God cannot or will not help you.

Very soon, discouragement will pry its way into your life. It usually hits a few days after you've decided to make a clean break with sin and develop habits of righteousness. Satan's line goes something like this: "You've tried to break this habit and failed. There is no reason to try again. You're not good enough to expect God to help you."

Another feeling you may have to battle is laziness—the notion that you need not put too much effort into the Christian life. You'll be tempted to procrastinate, to put off any serious attempt at seeking God's will concerning your problem. Satan never fears your good intentions. Only your obedience drives him to distraction.

Now take a hard look at your feelings and then ask yourself, "How can I cope with them?"

LOOK TO CHRIST'S EXAMPLE

Jesus Christ, as a man, experienced every human emotion. He wept at the grave of Lazarus. As He faced the indescribable assignment of bearing the sin of the world, He was traumatized by an excruciating emotional burden. Yet Jesus did not spend those last hours in self-pity, bemoaning His fate. He handled the experience constructively, and therefore provided a model for us all. What did He do?

First, He admitted His feelings: "My soul is deeply grieved, to the point of death; remain here and keep watch with Me" (Matt. 26:38). He allowed His disciples to have a glimpse of the unutterable passions that came upon Him in the dark. Suppressing feelings will not cause them to disappear. Feelings must be dealt with honestly; they should not be ignored. Needless to say, Jesus' emotional upheavals did not lead Him to sinful thoughts or behavior, but even so you must follow Him in honestly acknowledging how you feel. Admitting your bitterness, depression, hatred, or passion is the first step in learning to cope with your feelings.

We've all met people who will not admit to their feelings. A pastor once told of a deacon who, with a clenched fist and a flushed face, pounded on the table and, with fire in his eyes, shouted, "I'm not angry!"

A woman who recited in meticulous detail all of the wrongs her husband had committed against her ended her indictment with the startling statement, "Of course I'm not bitter; I've forgiven him for this!" But her careful cataloging of all the wrongs he had done betrayed her. Think of how often we are unwilling to admit how we really feel!

David, the psalmist, was vulnerably honest. Read his psalms, and you will be struck by the wide range of emotions that he felt. When he was joyful, he shouted praises; when he was depressed, he complained about God's silence and apparent indifference to his need. Depression, joy, and even anger were freely admitted. We don't know how often he told others about his woes, but we know he spent much time giving his problems to God. The first step, then, is to admit the truth about your emotions and tell God how you feel.

Second, Jesus requested the support of friends. He had three groups of disciples: the seventy who went from house to house to proclaim the kingdom, the twelve who were constantly with Him, and the three within that circle who were given special opportunities. Peter, James, and John, who had been invited to the Mount of Transfiguration, were asked to help their Master bear intense suffering. Jesus did not consider it beneath His dignity to ask His friends for prayerful intercession and companionship in the hour of trial.

Personally, I believe that many so-called emotional problems could be solved by corporate intercessory prayer. But the church today is much like the disciples who found praying more difficult than sleeping. Their spirit was willing, but their flesh was weak.

Third, Jesus knew that His emotional suffering would not separate Him from the Father's love and approval. Their relationship was not affected by the weight of His anguish. As believers we need to realize that our acceptance before God is unrelated to our feelings. We do not live the Christian life by moods, but by faith. Freedom comes to us when we understand that our walk with God is not dependent on how we feel when we get out of bed in the morning.

Finally, Jesus knew that blessing would follow obedience. Emotional peace and calm would come after doing God's will and not before. The assurance of joy in the future enabled Him to endure the tortures of the present. The author of Hebrews inspires us with the example of Jesus, telling us that as we pursue victory over the "sin which so easily entangles us" (Heb. 12:1), we can fix our "eyes on Jesus, who both began and finished this race we're in. Study how he did it. Because he never lost sight of where he was headed—that exhilarating finish in and with God—he could put up with anything along the way: Cross, shame, whatever. And now he's there, in the place of honor, right alongside God" (v. 2 MSG).

Remember that feelings flow from action and not vice versa. You can prove this fact tomorrow morning. If you follow your feelings, you will not get out of bed when the alarm clock rings. If you wait for the proper feeling your day will begin behind schedule. But if you choose to get up and start getting ready to go to work, whether you feel like it or not, you will soon discover that you are feeling pretty good. And by the time you have finished your breakfast, you will be thinking that life isn't so bad after all. Proper feelings come because of action; they do not precede the action itself.

Whenever we obey God, our feelings begin to fall in line. We have a sense of satisfaction, a sense of self-esteem. Feelings follow faith and obedience. Yet some Christians are still waiting for that magic moment when they will feel like obeying, feel like committing themselves to God, and feel like praying and reading their Bible!

Every one of us has tasks we dislike doing. What makes us think we should wait until we feel like doing them? Jesus did not feel like dying on the cross. He suffered more physical pain than we can ever comprehend, along with excruciating moral anguish, as the sinless One became identified with the sin of the world. Every emotional conflict known to man (except personal guilt) convulsed within the body of the Son of God. But He went ahead with God's will because He was obedient unto death, even the death of the cross (Phil. 2:8). Why did He do it? Jesus knew that after obedience there is joy. How often we have reversed the order. We think we've got to be in the right mood to obey God. But there is no joy until there is obedience.

One final word: We must learn to give thanks to God for all things, whether we feel like it or not. The focus of our attention must be the truth that is settled in heaven. Several years ago, I experienced a short period of depression. I learned in a matter of hours that depression is real; it's not just a fantasy. The evening it hit, life seemed useless. The phrase that kept popping into my head was, "Vanity of vanities! All is vanity" (Eccl. 1:2). I had always told others that the cure for depression was praise. It was time to take a dose of my own medicine.

Months before this incident, I had prepared a list of all the blessings that God has given us in Christ. Resisting all my negative emotional impulses, I began to thank God for each one. Even though I didn't feel thankful, I was grateful mentally, and I told God so. Even reciting the verses of Scripture and giving thanks seemed to be so futile. Yet I continued, resisting the thought of quitting. It wasn't long before the depression left. Of course, I'm not suggesting that all depression can be handled so simply. But in tackling our emotional moods, praise is the place to begin.

I've discovered a new liberty in my Christian life since realizing that my faith need not be tied to my feelings. We honor God when we walk by faith without emotional supports. And within time, our feelings begin to catch up with the truth that we accept with our minds. In practical terms, this means that you can begin right now to take constructive steps toward positive change. You'll never feel more like doing it than at this very moment. The questions at the end of this chapter will help you to begin right now.

QUESTIONS FOR SMALL GROUP STUDY OR PERSONAL REFLECTION

1. What evidence is there that our generation stresses physical comfort (feelings and pleasure) rather than a life of self-denial? Earlier in the chapter it was said that most sinful habits are developed by simply following the path of least resistance. Do you see evidence of this in your own life? In what areas? What can you do now to begin heading in another direction?

> Faith often runs counter to feeling. Even the attempt to find victory in feelings is a sin in the life of a believer. In short, it is simply "walking in the flesh." We must repent of the sin of assessing the reality of the Christ-life on the basis of feeling.
>
> —Henry Teichrob

2. Discuss this statement with questions such as these in mind: Why do our feelings fluctuate? Why do we so often think that spirituality is to be equated with "feeling just right"? Find some examples in Scripture where faith runs contrary to feelings.

3. Read the words of Jesus in John 12:27–28. How does the text show that His determination to do the Father's will often went counter to His own feelings? What duties do you have that you do not feel like

doing? Why then do you do them? What would happen if you only did whatever you felt like doing?

4. The author lists a series of steps to overcoming your feelings about a certain task or obstacle: First, you must admit your feelings. Second, you must ask for help from your friends and from God. Third, you must realize that your relationship with God is not dependent upon emotion—either yours or His. Finally, you must realize that blessing follows obedience. Spend some time now in prayer practicing these steps with regard to the stubborn habit you're trying to overcome.

5. What practical benefits are there in realizing that we walk by faith and not by emotional sight? Like the author, prepare a list of blessings that God has given you in Christ. Take some time now to thank the Lord for these blessings, and make it a habit to do so often.

Chapter 9

THE TAMING OF YOUR WILL

I just don't have any willpower!"
  We've all said those words, whether we were trying to lose weight, live by a budget, or fight an addiction. How frustrating to know what we ought to do and yet not have the strength to do it! The gap between knowledge and performance is often embarrassing. We just can't seem to get ourselves moving in the right direction. Yet, unless we can use our will effectively, we will always default to the same old habits and fall back into the same old behavioral ruts.

Can your will be disciplined? Yes. You do not need to drift aimlessly through life, carried along like a cork on a river. You can learn to make responsible decisions and say no to the path of least resistance.

WHAT IS YOUR WILL?

You might be wondering what you "will" is. Your will is your decision-making faculty. Often it is caught between your thoughts and your desires. Your emotions express how you feel, your mind says what you know, but your will decides the direction you will go. The weary disciples experienced this tension in Gethsemane. Jesus asked them twice to watch and pray with Him, but both times they fell asleep. Our Savior commented,

"Keep watching and praying that you may not enter into temptation; the spirit is willing, but the flesh is weak" (Matt. 26:41).

Now let's bring this subject a little closer to home—to your own bedroom, for instance. The alarm rings at 6:00 a.m., and your mind knows full well what that means: You should carefully move from a horizontal to a vertical position. But your body feels differently about the matter. Now your will has to make a decision that cannot satisfy both the body and the mind. And your will has only a few moments to decide to do so, or you will drift into unconscious comfort for another hour.

What determines whether your will follows the direction of the mind or the inclinations of the body? It depends on your desires and your determination to fulfill such desires. If your job is important to you, you'll be strongly inclined to get out of bed. If your temporary comfort is more attractive than a paycheck, you'll tend to ignore the alarm clock.

If you were born into a home with little discipline and weak commitment to dependability, you'll have a strong tendency to do whatever comes naturally. However, background cannot be used as an excuse for laziness, because those who were reared in well-disciplined homes fight the same natural desires. Believe it or not, we are all much the same inside!

Heredity also influences the will. We've all inherited tendencies from the temperaments of our parents. Those who have studied human nature believe they have discovered several distinct patterns. There are some things about us that will never change. To use a computer illustration: Our hardware never changes, but we can make changes to our software. Our basic traits may never change, but our attitude and behavior can be changed with God's help.

Think of what we have to overcome! Romans 3:10–11 reads, "There is none righteous, not even one; there is none who understands, there is none who seeks for God." Left to ourselves we would never seek God. He comes seeking us and changing our desires so that we might be better able to live up to what we know to be right and good.

Jesus taught that no one can come to Him unless drawn by the Father (John 6:44–65). God does not save us by circumventing our will. He works through our will, giving us the ability to choose to believe in Christ and also to do what is right. You have heard the expression, "Let go and let God," implying that God will take over and control us completely if we wish Him to do so. But this is not the teaching of Scripture. Our will does not become passive when we yield to God. A surrendered will experiences struggle, as Jesus' conflict in Gethsemane demonstrates.

Fortunately, the Holy Spirit does not stop working with our will at the time of conversion. Paul wrote, "For this purpose also I labor, striving according to His power, which mightily works within me" (Col. 1:29). The Holy Spirit stands ready to come to our aid the moment we face a temptation or a difficult decision.

THE BASIS OF CHOICE

Before you can bring your will into harmony with God's purposes you need the right goals for your life. If you don't believe that life is worth living, it won't make much difference to you whether you break sinful habits or reinforce them. A purposeful life, therefore, is the basis for discipline and determination to make right choices.

Day-to-day activities have short-term meaning. If you choose to clean the house, mow the lawn, or write a chapter of a book, you have a sense of satisfaction when the task is completed. Specific short-term goals give direction in how you use your time and can have long-term consequences.

But temporary goals are not adequate for a meaningful and satisfying life. An insurance executive who had achieved all the short-term goals imaginable—two beautiful homes, several luxury cars, and plenty of vacation time—committed suicide because "life wasn't worth the trouble of living." He had reached all of his material goals and found they were not ultimately satisfying. Only eternal values can give meaning to temporal ones. Time must be the servant of eternity. Let's look at how this truth can be applied to your life.

First, take the example of Moses. Moses could say no to the world because he was firmly convinced that time (or eternity, if you please) would vindicate his choice. Focusing on the eternal gave him the resources to make wise choices on earth.

Given his values, Moses was willing to forego immediate pleasures. The Bible does not deny there is pleasure in short-term goals. In Pharaoh's court, Moses could have enjoyed wine, women, and song, as well as far-flung political power. But he knew that such pleasures are short-lived. He was able to postpone his immediate desires because of his faith in future rewards. He could say no to the world without thinking he had been shortchanged.

In Hebrews 11, the record of the faithful ones, we read, "By faith, Moses, when grown, refused the privileges of the Egyptian royal house. He chose a hard life with God's people rather than an opportunistic soft life of sin with the oppressors. He valued suffering in the Messiah's camp far greater than Egyptian wealth because he was looking ahead, anticipating the payoff. By an act of faith, he turned his heel on Egypt, indifferent to the king's blind rage. He had his eye on the One no eye can see, and kept right on going" (Heb. 11:24–27 MSG).

Moses endured temporary hardship because he saw the Invisible One. He saw the difference between time and eternity. Paul wanted the Corinthian Christians to "look not at the things which are seen, but at the things which are not seen; for the things which are seen are temporal, but the things which are not seen are eternal" (2 Cor. 4:18).

Contrast the maturity of the church fathers, who understood the principle of delayed satisfaction, with the immaturity of the "now" generation, wanting all of its kicks, thrills, and highs at this very moment. No consideration is given to tomorrow, much less the distant future. The permanent is sacrificed on the altar of the immediate.

Those who trust God can postpone fulfillment of their desires. Sex can wait until marriage; the discipline of hard study can be endured for the sake of an education; and any sinful pleasure can be abandoned in favor of the greater pleasure of fellowship with God. The question then, is not whether we will have pleasure, but which pleasure we will have: The fleeting and ultimately unsatisfying pleasures of sin or the lasting pleasures of God?

Now let's look at the example of Jesus Christ. Jesus knew where He had come from, why He was here, and what He was supposed to accomplish. He came down from heaven, not to do His own will, but the will of the Father. That determination controlled every decision He made. As a result, He was not distracted with the trivial. He was never in a hurry, for He knew His Father would not initiate a task without allotting the time to complete it. He was not driven by crises, feeling He had to heal everyone in Israel. He could say, "It is finished," even when many people were still bound by demons and twisted by disease. What mattered ultimately was not the number of people healed or fed, but whether the Father's will was being done. His clearly defined goals simplified His decisions.

We, too, need such a singleness of purpose. Dr. Ari Kiev of the Cornell Medical Center states, "Observing the lives of people who have mastered adversity, I have repeatedly noted that they have established goals and, irrespective of obstacles, have sought with all their effort to achieve them. From the moment they've fixed an objective in their minds and decided to concentrate all their energies on a specific goal, they begin to surmount the most difficult odds."

We must stop putting first-rate value on third-rate priorities. We need to establish once for all that our goal is to please our Father in heaven. Once we repent of our idolatries and know that God is our goal, it is much easier to make the right decisions. Indeed, the journey becomes a pleasure.

How Do We Set Goals?

The invisible is more valuable than the visible. The eternal is more enduring than the temporal. But what do these facts have to do with our values, our goals? Our goals are set on the foundation of our larger beliefs about life and about ourselves. Within the framework of our ultimate commitments we formulate our short-range goals.

Let me suggest three levels of commitment that are appropriate for the Christian: (1) a commitment to God in Christ, (2) a commitment to the body of Christ, and (3) a commitment to the work God has given us to do. These three levels are the outline in which you can specify what you want to accomplish with your life. It is your responsibility to creatively spell out how you plan to fulfill these goals. For example, your commitment to God might mean that you spend half an hour each day getting to know the One to whom you have committed yourself. You may want to cut the time you spend watching TV, or even cancel your cable subscription.

You will want to set goals in other parts of your life too.

You may want to lose some excess pounds. A body redeemed by God should be healthy. Once you decide how much weight you plan to lose and the diet you will follow—stay with it! Choose to forego immediate desires. When you are tempted by foods that are not part of your diet, remind yourself that this immediate pleasure can be postponed. Your goal to honor God should mean more to you than the craving for excess food. But be careful that such a diet—or any other commitment—does not become a god unto itself. God desires a healthy balance for our lives.

Of course, the value of such discipline will reach into such everyday activities as getting out of bed in the morning, carrying out the garbage, or washing windows. You can bring your body under control and do what is in line with the person you hope to become. If you value your commitments to God, then make sure that your yes and your no are consistent with your long-term goals.

Your momentary feelings are not a good guide toward fulfilling desirable goals. Paul had his body in control: "I don't know about you, but I'm running hard for the finish line. I'm giving it everything I've got. No sloppy living for me! I'm staying alert and in top condition. I'm not going to get caught napping, telling everyone else all about it and then missing out myself" (1 Cor. 9:27 MSG). You simply cannot give in to all the desires of your body. You would be dead in less than a week if you did!

SURRENDERING TO GOD IS DIFFICULT

It is good to set priorities, to have goals. But what about your "want-to"? Your will? How are you going to hold to these goals you are setting that fit into your belief about God's desire for your life?

Setting good goals is not easy. And staying with them is even harder. As a Christian you need the help of God as you seek to do His will. And yet it is just at this point that conflict arises.

The struggle between our own selfish will and God's will is intense. We've learned that we were born with the desire to control our own destinies, to do our own thing. Consequently, our fallen will is adept at making choices in harmony with our pride, independence, and self-determination. We resist the idea that God should rule over us, particularly when He begins to meddle in our private affairs.

Perhaps you don't want God to decide whether or not you have a marriage partner. You don't want to submit your plans to a higher authority for approval. If you want to spend your Sunday afternoon watching football, that ought to be your decision. Or if you are skimpy in giving your money to the local church, that is your business. Entrusting yourself wholly to God seems rather impractical. If you don't take care of yourself, who will? You have to look out for ol' number one!

It is just this kind of attitude that shows the need to learn obedience and humility. Usually we think that the human will must be strengthened, but paradoxically we become stronger only when we become weaker. When we surrender our will to God, we finally discover the resources to do what God requires. As we give ourselves to Him, trusting His promises, we receive His power.

When we are at the end of our rope, God is there to catch us—but not before. David knew that the most he could offer God was a yielded will, "The sacrifices of God are a broken spirit; a broken and a contrite heart, O God, You will not despise" (Ps. 51:17). Submission to God always involves humility; it is an acknowledgment that we are neither qualified nor able to do what we ought to do. The temptation to strive with the Almighty is ever with us.

A businessman woke up early one Sunday morning and went golfing with friends. He knew there was a men's meeting at the church, part of a revival that was in progress. When he finished playing eighteen holes, it was noon. His curiosity made him stop at the church on his way home. He hoped the meeting would be over. But if not, he would at least "check to see who was there." To his amazement, half of the men were on their knees, many of them weeping. Others had left the room for special prayer.

He let all of this spiritual activity register for a moment and then angrily clenched his fist and slammed it into his other hand, and said, "You'll never get me, God!"

Get him for what? What would make a Christian say such a thing? The matter most pressing on his mind was his relationship with his children. The man was victimized by a hot temper, and many times he had hurt his children's feelings and wounded their spirits. He knew that if God "got" him, he would have to humble himself and ask the forgiveness of his children. He decided that the price was too great.

When we fight against the demands of God, trying to weasel out of whatever doesn't suit us, our will is pitted against His in a desperate struggle for survival. But when we say yes to God, we discover the ability to do His will. Strength is dependent upon surrender.

God did "get" the businessman. He humbled himself and went to his children to ask their forgiveness. Later, as he told how God had broken him, he wept unashamedly. God gave him the willpower to do what he could not do on his own. And his will was energized by the Holy Spirit when he stopped resisting and chose to say no to his sin. At that point it became possible for God to work through the man's will to accomplish His purpose.

YOU CAN LESSEN THE CONFLICT

Does temptation ever lose its power? Not completely. Even when we are motivated by a desire to please God we experience conflict because God often requires obedience that runs counter to human motivations. Jesus Himself expressed this conflict: "For I have come down from heaven, not to do My own will but the will of Him who sent Me" (John 6:38). He voluntarily set aside any personal ambitions and submitted Himself to His Father's will.

The conflict between your immediate interests and God's long-range goals is never just going to go away. But there is an answer. For when you begin to commit yourself to God, the Holy Spirit begins to resolve these conflicts. He pulls the fragments of your life together. He shows you His truth as a standard for making choices. He teaches you a single-mindedness that you never knew before. He shows you the rewards of living in His love and justice. And after a while, you begin to realize that in many instances, what God requires of you is really what you want to do. Just as the psalmist wrote, "Delight yourself in the LORD; and He will give you the desires of your heart" (Ps. 37:4).

This helps us understand Jesus' conflict. True, His human inclinations ran contrary to what the Father's will required. Paul says that Jesus did not please Himself (Rom. 15:3). But His satisfaction in doing God's will was much greater than the natural desire to avoid suffering. The prophet predicted that Christ would say, "I delight to do Your will, O my God" (Ps. 40:8).

Visualize a piece of steel suspended between two magnets. It vacillates, swinging from the right to the left or vice versa. For a moment, it wavers. It could go either way, because it is being simultaneously drawn in two directions by two powerful forces. After wavering for a second, it begins to move in one direction or the other. Then it moves more rapidly, unable to swing back any more. It is out of the range of the other magnet's power.

You may be hovering between God and the world. Sometimes you follow your own desires, sometimes God's. No one knows what your eventual decision will be. But the farther you go in God's direction, the less attraction the world will have. The day will come when your choices will be easier. Saying yes to God can be habit forming.

There is another lesson you can learn from this illustration. You can't say no to temptation unless you say yes to God. Like the magnet, the world will never lose its power to attract. To merely resist its power is pointless; no will is strong enough. But if you focus your attention on God as revealed in the Scriptures, you remove yourself from the sphere of the world's influence.

I have found that I can't resist enticing thoughts simply by saying, "I resist that thought!" The thought returns again and again. I do, however, have the ability to switch my thoughts to the Scriptures—quote a verse, offer praise, or renew my fellowship with God. Only in the presence of the Almighty does the world lose its allure.

God has given us the resources to say no to sin. Paul urged his readers to obey, but not merely by appealing to their unaided human wills. He reminded them that "it is God who is at work in you, both to will and to work for His good pleasure" (Phil. 2:13). God works in us by energizing our will. He helps us make the decisions that we ought to make, and ultimately really want to make.

God uses our struggles with temptation to teach us how to depend on His power. The ninth fruit of the Spirit is self-control (Gal. 5:23). That word, *self-control*, means literally "to hold oneself in." It refers to the mastery of desires—in the interest of higher ideals.

Don't feel powerless against a barrage of temptations. Maybe you have an insatiable desire for drugs, alcohol, or sex. Maybe your sins are restricted to your mind. Whatever your sins, there is hope. Like Jesus, Moses, and an innumerable host of saints before you, you can eventually say no to any stubborn habit, by setting the right priorities. And the more you learn to love Christ, the less you will be attracted by the world.

QUESTIONS FOR GROUP STUDY
OR PERSONAL REFLECTION

1. Read Psalm 73, written by Asaph, who began to wonder whether serving God was worthwhile. Notice particularly how his problem was solved when he began to focus on eternal rather than temporal rewards. What temporal things in your own life could you do with a little less of in order to embrace a little more eternity? Write them down.

2. Ponder Proverbs 25:28. Describe the characteristics of someone who has no control over his spirit. What are the advantages of being disciplined?

3. Take an inventory of your life by asking: In what areas am I resisting God's complete ownership? Suggested areas might be: schedule, pleasures, recreation, vocation, health, reputation, marital status, friendships, computer time, to name a few. Pray right now and give these areas fully to God.

4. Take some time now to make a list of your short- and long-term goals according to the levels of commitment laid out earlier in the chapter: (1) a commitment to God in Christ, (2) a commitment to the body of Christ, and (3) a commitment to the work God has given you to do.

5. If you have not already done so, set aside twenty minutes each morning to begin the day with God. You'll be tempted not to follow through with your commitment. Write down what those temptations might be and develop a strategy to combat them.

Chapter 10

THE INTERCESSION OF CHRIST AND BELIEVERS

I'm sometimes reminded of a horse we had on our farm growing up. He walked into a slough on his own, but had to be pulled out by a tractor! Just like my horse, it is possible for us to develop the worst habits on our own, but we need help getting out of the behavioral ruts.

One summer day, I ate lunch with a man who has been helping men say no to Internet pornography. I was expecting him to give me some new spiritual truth I had not previously known so I could pass it on to those who struggle. To my surprise, he said the most helpful piece of advice for men is to join a small group of other men for Bible study and prayer. Through interpersonal relationships and accountability, God honors the humility and faithfulness of those who stand together in overcoming temptations and sins.

The body of Christ is not just powerful to help its members overcome stubborn habits. It also can help those who are experiencing spiritual defeat of any kind—depression, for instance.

Susan was planning to die on August 22. She had been a believer for twelve years and had no doubt that she was God's child. She taught Sunday school, witnessed, and tried to live "a good Christian life."

But she was still experiencing prolonged periods of depression. Her health was failing, and pressures in the home had become unbearable. Two of her older children were rebellious, and Susan couldn't cope with it all. She had looked to her husband for support and felt that he was insensitive and cold; he just didn't understand what she was going through. She read books to find an answer, but nothing seemed to help. Her only relief was through tranquilizers and sleeping pills. She felt she was alone in the struggle and no one else could help her.

Her next step was to contemplate divorce. She recalls, "I wanted out—fast." Her husband had recently committed himself to Christ at a meeting in their home church. Susan was glad; he needed it. But now she began to think her husband didn't love her anymore. He just walked around with a smile on his face, completely relaxed, and seemed more insensitive than ever.

Susan had had enough of everything, including life itself. She awoke on August 22 and meticulously planned her last day on earth: She would help her sixteen-year-old son get his driving permit and perhaps even straighten out a few things in the house. Her sleeping pills were with her. She was at peace, confident she had made the right decision.

When she arrived back home with her son, she went to change clothes. "Where are you going?" her son asked. "To the ladies' meeting at the church," she answered thoughtlessly. "Do you have to?" he responded.

Susan did not want to go, but decided that she would. Unusual events had been going on at the church; in fact, a revival was in progress. The ladies were having a special meeting. Still confident that this would be her last day on earth, she cried the four miles to the church. "Lord," she prayed, "I know John will be better off with a new wife; the children will be better off with a different mother."

Trembling, she entered the sanctuary. The smiles on the women's faces only amplified her own depression. She did not participate in the singing. Instead, she wept for fifteen minutes.

When the group stopped for lunch, she would not eat. She had been without food for four days and didn't plan to eat now. A woman invited her to come to the prayer room for some counsel and prayer. Susan's struggle was intense. She had not planned on confessing her sins and yielding herself to God. But four other women joined her; they read the Scriptures with her and then they began to pray. There on their knees, the women interceded for Susan. An hour passed before the long ordeal was over. When Susan emerged from the prayer room she recalls that she "had no thought of death. I had never felt so alive in all my life."

Six months later she wrote, "Even though Satan has buffeted me a number of times, I can say that God does all things well, because truly His power is shown in weakness. I do have a health problem—but the depression is gone."

Susan's experience illustrates an important biblical principle: We cannot successfully live the Christian life on our own. God never intended that any one of us experience either failure or success alone, independent of the body of Christ. We need God's people for encouragement and intercession, and for the strength that comes from close fellowship.

And perhaps more important, we need the intercession of Christ. Our sin is never a private matter. We cannot say, "It only hurts me." God, Christ, and Satan are all involved in our failures, whether public or private. Satan accuses us before the Father, the Son intercedes for us, and the Father gives the verdict. Lewis Sperry Chafer used to say, "A secret sin on earth is an open scandal in heaven."

THE INTERCESSION OF CHRIST

Whenever tragedy strikes a family, the people who can be of most comfort are those who have had a similar experience. A widow can be of comfort to another widow; bereaved parents are helped by the support of others who have lost a child. There are two reasons. First, it's encouraging to know that others have survived a similar difficulty. Second, all of us want to meet someone who knows how we feel.

Christ qualifies on both counts. He experienced every temptation we've ever encountered. He was assaulted by Satan and hounded by physical distress. He faced hunger, rejection, and death successfully. And today, He is deeply moved by our own feelings and struggles. The excruciating pain of the cross, coupled with the horror of being identified with sin, was more torment than we could ever bear. That's why the Scriptures can say, "We don't have a high priest who is out of touch with our reality. He's been through weakness and testing, experienced it all—all but the sin" (Heb. 4:15 MSG). Today He says to us, "I know how you feel." Furthermore, He is moved with compassion—sympathy, if you please—for our weaknesses.

Can we confront Satan and win? Can we experience death and arrive safely on the other side? Jesus did, and in Him we can too! Because He endured His temptations, He offers all of us hope. Today He is at the right hand of God the Father, making intercession for us (Rom. 8:34). His presence reminds the Father that we have been bought at high cost. When we sin, He takes up our case and assumes all of the legal aspects of our relationship with God (1 John 2:1).

An example of His power of intercession is seen in the life of Simon-Peter. After the Lord's Supper was instituted, Jesus said to him, "Simon, stay on your toes. Satan has tried his best to separate all of you from me, like chaff from wheat. Simon, I've prayed for you in particular that you not give in or give out. When you have come through the time of testing, turn to your companions and give them a fresh start" (Luke 22:31–32 MSG).

Peter retorted, "Lord, with You I am ready to go both to prison and to death!" (v. 33). Jesus was not impressed. He knew that hours later Peter would deny Him as his courage turned to cowardice.

Was Jesus' prayer answered? Yes! Peter did deny Him, but the story doesn't end there. It says, "He went out and wept bitterly" (v. 62). After his repentance, he was able to comfort and strengthen others. His ministry, as recorded in the book of Acts, and his letters to the young and suffering church, are proof that Jesus' prayer was answered.

Satan sifted Peter and discovered that he was part chaff and part wheat. But because of the intercession of Jesus, the chaff was blown away, and the wheat became nourishment for others in need. God gives Satan permission to do the same to us. Temptation, struggles, and failures are all part of the process. Most of us, like Peter, are a mixture of chaff and wheat, as our track record shows. But our Lord is qualified to keep us from stumbling irrevocably. "For since He Himself was tempted in that which He has suffered, He is able to come to the aid of those who are tempted" (Heb. 2:18).

What an encouragement! Think again about that sin in your life that you can't seem to conquer. The outcome of that struggle is intensely important to God. It's a contest between Christ and Satan, and you happen to be the trophy!

But Christ is not the only one who intercedes for us. He invites all believers to participate in this rewarding ministry. Remember Jesus' intercession in Gethsemane? He was struggling with the prospect of the cross and asked His disciples to watch with Him. Three times He asked them to participate in His agony. They failed because they were too weary, but the invitation was there. Christ gives us the same opportunity. We can intercede with Him on behalf of other believers. We're invited to join Him in a ministry of intercession.

THE INTERCESSION OF BELIEVERS

Sometimes our besetting sin won't budge until we enlist the prayer support of God's people, particularly in the case of addiction to alcohol, drugs, or sexual misconduct. We need the added support of others who will stand for us in the presence of God. Recently, after I had spoken at a church meeting, a young woman struggling with homosexual behavior came up to talk to me. She was feeling morally weak; in fact, she wasn't even sure she wanted to change her lifestyle. Clearly she needed the persistent prayers and encouragement of God's people to help her come to terms with her problem.

Why is this necessary? Why doesn't an all-powerful God just give us victory if we individually apply the right principles? On the surface, it seems odd that our failure or success should be determined by other believers' faithfulness or negligence. Why the need for others to become involved in our personal affairs?

Primarily, it is because God wants us to give up our independent spirit. By nature, we are creatures who prefer to live according to our own blueprint. How we live is our business—what right does anyone have to ask or even be interested in how we are progressing spiritually? If we want them to know, we'll tell them!

The New Testament teaches otherwise. We are all members of the body of Christ, and each of us affects the function of others. If you have ever had a toothache, you know that the parts of your body are not isolated. When one tooth aches, your whole body hurts.

Have you ever seen a human hand severed from a body? It looks gruesome. Yet, attached to an arm and connected to the nervous system, the hand is not only highly useful, but beautiful, too. The difference lies in its relationship to the body. Similarly, in Christ no individual is anything if cut off from the body.

That's why God wants us to enlist the resources of other believers. It's humbling to realize that we need their support and help, but we do. Our struggles and temptations remind us that successes or failures are always a team effort. There's no room in the body of Christ for an individual scorecard. And the pride that keeps us from being honest with one another has to be broken.

That's why we must be acquainted with God's people. We must form friendships in church, where committed believers gather for fellowship and instruction. Within the larger circle of believers, we'll find that some will become special friends. As we develop confidence in them, we can turn to them in our time of need. At that moment, we are tapping a reservoir of spiritual power. Jesus said, "When two or three of you are together because of me, you can be sure that I'll be there" (Matt. 18:20 MSG). The first responsibility of God's people is persistent prayer for one another; not merely individual prayer, but corporate prayer. Prayer as a group is important.

Recently, I talked to a couple who was deeply hurt because a child they had adopted was taken away from them by the child's natural mother. Hopelessly neurotic and bitter, the biological mother had found her son and kidnapped him. Understandably, this Christian couple, who had accepted this boy from birth, was deeply upset. "Everyone is praying for us, but there's been no break in the case," the distraught woman told me. When I asked if people met with them for prayer, she responded, "No, but they all say they are praying for us." My suggestion to her was that they select a group of people, perhaps six, to meet with them regularly for prayer. It's not enough for people to say, "We're praying." There is supportive value in sharing our heartbreaks with a group of God's people. Jesus, you will recall, wanted the disciples to be at His side during His agony in Gethsemane. It wasn't only their prayers that He wanted. He wanted companionship during those agonizing moments, to give and receive encouragement.

A second way others can help is by keeping us responsible and accountable. We can agree to report to a group, or at least to one individual, on spiritual progress. If I know someone is going to ask me, "How's that problem coming?" I'm going to be more inclined to flee from temptation. One man suggested to his friend, "Whenever you are tempted to take another drink, call my cell phone, any time of day, and we'll pray together."

When I was in seminary, a close friend of mine and I met together for sharing and prayer every Thursday evening at nine thirty. We were able to be honest with each other and give reports on our failures and successes. Knowing about that appointment was an incentive for me to keep watch on my actions so that I would not let my friend down. Of course, when we do fail, we need to be honest. Our pride will urge us say that all is well when it is not. But when we develop responsibility toward others, it helps us do what we ought.

This practice of checking on each other can be used in many different ways. Recently, another friend of mine and I agreed to learn the essential teaching of one chapter of the Bible every day. Occasionally, we call each other on the telephone just to check on how we are doing. "What's in chapter 12?" he'll ask, and I've got to know it cold. When I'm tempted to let the project slide, I remind myself of that commitment and how I'd feel if I were to fail his quiz.

A man who struggled with homosexuality once told me that he would not go downtown without the companionship of another Christian. The man simply did not trust himself. The temptation to cruise and slide back into his former ways was too strong. But with a Christian companion along, he would not succumb to such enticement. Later, when he became stronger spiritually, he did not need such support.

God wants to teach us that we cannot live a successful Christian life independent of His children. If we are wayward, we must be restored; if we are weak, others must share their strength with us. At no time should we begin to think that we can make it alone with God—for we need His redeemed people, too.

RESTORING A BELIEVER

What should we do when we see a fellow believer trapped in a sinful habit? Discuss the matter with our friends? Or do nothing, hoping that someday he or she will snap out of it?

The Bible is explicit about our responsibility. If a believer has erred, and not merely violated our personal preferences, it is our responsibility to restore him or her, and bring the person to a right relationship with God. Jesus instructed, "If a fellow believer hurts you, go and tell him—work it out between the two of you. If he listens, you've made a friend. If he won't listen, take one or two others along so that the presence of witnesses will keep things honest, and try again. If he still won't listen, tell the church. If he won't listen to the church, you'll have to start over from scratch, confront him with the need for repentance, and offer again God's forgiving love" (Matt. 18:15–17 MSG).

Our first responsibility is to go to that individual in private. We shouldn't tell our friends, our relatives, or even our pastor! At this point, there is no reason to make the sin public. If the brother or sister is repentant and is given instruction on how to break from their sin, there is no reason for others to become involved.

We've all disobeyed God on this score. Confronting another believer in love takes courage, so we prefer the cowardly route of gossip. We pass the news to others, thinking they should help, or at least "pray." Baser motives often lie beneath such excuses. We delight in other people's faults because it gives us an exalted feeling of superiority. "I'd never do that."

Churches split and family relationships are shattered beyond repair because believers do not have the courage to go to a fellow Christian caught in a sin. Matters that should be cared for in private mushroom into bitter confrontations when people choose sides on the issues. Such is the price of cowardice. More accurately, such is the fruit of disobedience.

Paul gave some instructions regarding our attitude in the restoration process. If the person's sin is generally known, the church should select qualified members to confront the believer in love. "Live creatively, friends. If someone falls into sin, forgivingly restore him, saving your critical comments for yourself. You might be needing forgiveness before the day's out" (Gal. 6:1 MSG). We've already mentioned that sin in another person's life tends to generate self-righteousness in us. We like to feel superior and believe we are immune to similar temptation. That type of an attitude will stifle any attempt to restore a believer. Paul warns that we dare not come across as super-Christians. We must go in humility, knowing full well that we could slide into the same trespass.

Of course, the initial contact is not the end of the matter. We must be prepared to befriend, counsel, and pray with those who hurt. God wants every one of us to have a ministry in the life of another believer. I don't mean that this ministry must be one-sided; we'll soon discover that we cannot help others without being edified in return. We all need to be dependent on each other. Anything less fosters individualism, which within the church is sin.

Do you need help spiritually? Connect with other imperfect believers and become a mutual support system. God will most probably not let you break those stubborn habits on your own.

QUESTIONS FOR GROUP STUDY
OR PERSONAL REFLECTION

1. Read 1 Corinthians 12. What responsibility does one member of the body of Christ have to another? Give specific examples. Why do you think that believers do not help each other as they ought?

2. Do you currently have anyone that you meet with on a regular basis to discuss spiritual growth? What would such a relationship look like to you? If you haven't already, try to become a member of a small group of believers who pray together and support one another spiritually. Learn to share your concerns and struggles with them. Think of creative ways that the group could better help one another grow in Christ. Write them down.

3. In what ways have churches often given the impression that they are not interested in helping those with special needs? What can be done to change this impression —or fact?

4. How often do you allow Christ to enter into your trials and temptations? The Bible tells us it is because of Christ we have access to the Father (John 16:23-27). So take some time right now to thank Jesus for what He did on the cross, and ask Him to participate in your struggles freely.

Chapter 11

SATANIC ACTIVITY

The devil has already made meticulous plans for our downfall. Behind the lies we want so desperately to believe is the Liar. He wants to run our behavioral ruts so deep that we can no longer say no to a habit, no matter how destructive it might be. Whether it's gambling, alcoholism, or a sexual addiction of some kind, our enemy wants to tighten the cords that bind us.

A recent survey showed that Americans are addicted to the media: the Internet, TV, movies, video games, cell phones, and other gadgets that can quickly lead to obsessive-compulsive behavior. More people than we realize develop an insatiable appetite for these kinds of amusements—an appetite that they can neither satisfy nor change. The media industry is Satan's playground. He uses it to distract us from what is really important as he attempts to turn us into robots who obey our appetites no matter how destructive they may be.

We must believe that satanic forces are involved in our spiritual struggles. Some Christians teach that the only time we confront satanic activity is in cases of bizarre behavior or dabbling in the occult. However, I believe that satanic powers can play a part in any sin that crops up in the routine of daily living. It's just that Satan prefers to work undercover.

Let's take lying as an example. Most Christians who tell an occasional lie would never suspect that Satan has anything to do with it. They may tell a "white lie" to wiggle out of an embarrassing circumstance or to protect their reputation. Surely such behavior has no connection with Satan!

But consider the case of Ananias and Sapphira, mentioned in Acts 5. You'll recall they lied about the amount of money they received from the sale of their land. Let's assume they sold their land for $1,000, but when asked how much they got for it, they said $600. In one sense, they spoke the truth—they had sold it for $600, though they failed to say it was $600 plus $400! That is a white lie—what some people call a *trivial* white lie.

Who would have guessed that Satan was the instigator of this deception? Yet, Peter confronted the husband and said, "Ananias, why has Satan filled your heart to lie to the Holy Spirit and to keep back some of the price of the land?" (Acts 5:3). Later when his wife, Sapphira, came in, Peter also confronted her and said, "Why is it that you have agreed together to put the Spirit of the Lord to the test?" (v. 9). When Ananias and Sapphira had a discussion and agreed to tell a lie, they never realized that the Devil had actually inserted a lie into their mind; they credited themselves with the idea.

Does Satan play a role in the breakup of a marriage? Paul warns that couples ought to meet one another's sexual needs, "so that Satan will not tempt you because of your lack of self-control" (1 Cor. 7:5). Again, Satan is there, doing whatever he can to ruin a marriage.

Let us suppose that your sin is cowardice. You just can't seem to open your mouth for Christ. You feel awkward and embarrassed to be identified with Him. Could these fears be instigated by the Devil? When Peter denied Jesus, our Lord remarked that it was Satan who demanded that Peter be sifted as wheat (Luke 22:31). Yes, Satan was actively involved in Peter's denial of Christ. The Evil One also hindered Paul from visiting the church at Thessalonica (1 Thess. 2:18). He is the originator of false doctrine, and the deceived are "held captive by him to do his will" (2 Tim. 2:26). Satan obscures the issues of the gospel and blinds the minds of the unsaved "that they might not see the light of the gospel of the glory of Christ, who is the image of God" (2 Cor. 4:4). Also, Satan causes people to forget the Word of God by taking information out of their minds so that they will not be saved (Luke 8:12).

You may think you have never met a person who has had any contact with demonic forces. But you've met yourself, and I suspect that is sufficient. No one can escape contact with "the prince of the power of the air" (Eph. 2:2 KJV), the one who has organized his army of wicked spirits to fight God's people.

SATAN'S TARGET

For centuries, philosophers and scientists have struggled with the problem of the nature of the mind. They have wrestled with questions such as: What are thoughts? What is the relationship between mind and body? But this much seems clear: Thoughts do not occupy space as we know it but exist in a separate realm. For example, it would be absurd to speak of a thought as a quarter-inch long, or as occupying a specified area. Because thoughts exist in a spiritual realm, it's safe to say that the mind is vulnerable to spiritual influences as well.

The spiritual part of human beings exists in a realm that is not off-limits to spiritual forces, whether good or evil. We've already learned that it was the Devil who gave Ananias and Sapphira the idea to lie about the sale of their land. Where do you think Judas got the idea to betray Jesus? John said that the Devil put the suggestion into his heart (John 13:2). The mind is a target for satanic attack.

Satan loves exploiting our areas of weakness. He delights in influencing our passions, arousing our greed and anger, inflating our egos, and stirring up our hatred and resentment. All of this and more is done by the roaring lion who stalks the earth, "seeking whom he may devour" (1 Peter 5:8 KJV). We can be sure he is involved in our besetting sin.

Does his activity absolve us from any responsibility in committing sin? Not in the least. Peter did not let Ananias and Sapphira off the hook because their lie was instigated by Satan, and Judas was responsible for his betrayal of Jesus. If we allow satanic activity in our life, God will hold us responsible because we have the power to choose whether we will pursue Satan's suggestions. Yes, Satan might suggest that we lie, but the choice of whether to act on that suggestion is ours. He may tease us with any sin imaginable, but ultimately you and I make the choice. He cannot work independent of our cooperation.

DEALING WITH THE DEVIL

Some Christians reason, "If I leave Satan alone, he'll leave me alone. I don't want to get involved." Without realizing it, these believers have unwittingly conceded the battle to the enemy. Satan has them exactly where he wants them, safely tucked away on the shelf labeled "Too Frightened to Fight." I tell such people, "You don't want to get involved? My friends, you are involved—you've just made peace with the enemy by refusing to do battle with him."

Satan's most successful weapon is fear. He'll make you believe that if you take his existence seriously, he will create havoc in your home or ruin your peace of mind. Don't believe him. Satan "is a liar and the father of lies" (John 8:44). He will bluff you, push you as far as your ignorance will allow. But as a believer, you have the authority to renounce Satan's foothold in your life.

First, you must take inventory and check your armor. If there is one piece missing, you are vulnerable. That exposed area is exactly where the arrow will be aimed! Satan is an expert marksman. His arrows don't miss their target; you can't depend on a sloppy defense to get you by unscathed. This is one war in which good luck doesn't count.

We can't discuss all seven pieces of armor here, but they are listed in Ephesians 6:12–17. Let me comment on only one: the breastplate of righteousness. Satan always needs some reason to trouble us, some sin that gives him a right to our life. Once that sin is confessed and forsaken, his foothold disintegrates. He still will attack, but we need not fall for his enticements.

I've counseled people who feel uncomfortable when someone even mentions the blood of Jesus. Most often they will not even look me in the eye, but try to shy away. Usually, it is because they have wandered into Satan's territory by refusing to deal thoroughly with their past sins. Righteousness shields us from demonic attack. Satanic arrows are deflected when our conscience is void of offense. If you are troubled by satanic attack, you should ask yourself: Where have I given ground to Satan? What sins do I tolerate? Where do I resist God? Personal righteousness, then, is essential in sealing yourself off from Satan's activity. But so are the other pieces of armor listed in Ephesians. They are numbered at the end of this chapter for your study.

Second, you need to realize that Satan has no rights, but won't admit it. Jesus' death and ascension effectively cut the ground from under him. Before His death, Jesus predicted, "Now judgment is upon this world; now the ruler of this world will be cast out" (John 12:31). Jesus' death and ascension to heaven won a legal victory over all satanic forces—Jesus Christ beat Satan on his home turf. Paul wrote regarding Christ, "He stripped all the spiritual tyrants in the universe of their sham authority at the Cross and marched them naked through the streets" (Col. 2:15 MSG). That's why James could write, "Let God work his will in you. Yell a loud no to the Devil and watch him scamper" (4:7 MSG). Satan is allowed to maneuver through the atmosphere, causing havoc. But he can be successfully resisted.

Paul wrote, "Go ahead and be angry. You do well to be angry—but don't use your anger as fuel for revenge. And don't stay angry. Don't go to bed angry. Don't give the Devil that kind of foothold in your life" (Eph. 4:26–27 MSG).

Satan is like a dethroned king who keeps on giving orders to his subjects; he is like a thief who has stolen virtually everything you own and who tries to persuade you that it was always his. He is like a warrior without authority who keeps recruiting mercenaries to fight a battle he has already lost! You *can* say no to Satan!

Finally, remember that all believers have legal authority over demonic forces. There is a connection between Ephesians 1 and 2 that is often overlooked. Near the end of the first chapter we read of God's great power, which was displayed in Christ:

> God raised him from death and set him on a throne in
> deep heaven, in charge of running the universe, every-
> thing from galaxies to governments, no name and no
> power exempt from his rule. And not just for the time
> being, but forever. He is in charge of it all, has the final
> word on everything. At the center of all this, Christ rules
> the church. The church, you see, is not peripheral to the
> world; the world is peripheral to the church. The church
> is Christ's body, in which he speaks and acts, by which he
> fills everything with his presence. (Eph. 1:20–23 MSG)

I hope you read these verses carefully enough to see (1) that Christ's ascension to heaven placed Him above all rule, authority, power, "and every name that is named" (v. 21 KJV), and (2) that "all things [are] under His feet" (v. 22 KJV)—no power exists in the universe without Christ's permission.

And here is the good news that pulls it all together: In chapter 2, verse 6, Paul says we are seated with Christ in heavenly places. This means that Satan, along with all of his wicked spirits, at this very moment is under our feet!

Often we feel weak and helpless, but this does not diminish our position of authority. A policeman may not feel strong at all; indeed, he may be ill or exhausted. Physically, he would not be able to stop the smallest compact car; yet when he raises his hand, all the traffic stops. Why? Because the government has given him authority over traffic.

Some people have told me, "I hear voices that tell me to commit suicide. I'm afraid that one of these days I will do it." You and I need not listen to such voices! Satan likes to make people think that he can program them and that they must obey his commands. Christ's death and ascension have put an end to such lies. The message of the New Testament is clear: Christ won a complete victory over Satan, and believers now participate in that triumph.

DEMONIC ACTIVITY AND YOUR SINFUL HABIT

How do you confront wicked powers? Follow the example of Jesus, who commanded, "Go, Satan! For it is written …" (Matt. 4:10). Use this formula, out loud if you are alone, and command Satan to depart, based on the promises of Scripture that you have claimed. Earlier in this book we talked about the need for memorizing verses of Scripture that relate directly to temptations. Of course, shouting a verse of Scripture at demonic powers in and of itself does not make them cringe. In the temptation of Christ, Satan retorted with a verse of his own. The power of the Word of God is unleashed when you bring yourself under its authority.

Although the disciples were given authority to expel demons, they discovered they were not always able to do so (Luke 9:1–6, 37–43). At times they found themselves powerless because they had allowed the sin of unbelief to grow in their lives (Matt. 17:19–21). Furthermore, they were concerned about their own reputations and places in the kingdom of heaven. Jesus rebuked them for arguing about who would be the greatest among them (Luke 9:46–50). They were ineffective because their lives were no longer under God's authority.

God has given us the right to deal with demonic forces as long as we are under His authority. To put it simply, only those who are under authority can exercise authority. Satan and his forces must eventually back away when confronted by an obedient child of the living God who makes bold use of biblical truth. So don't be afraid to confront satanic forces directly when you are wrestling with those sinister thoughts that refuse to leave.

Let me warn you that you may lose many battles, but eventually you will win the war. Slowly your victories will begin to outnumber your defeats. You'll discover that you do have authority, just as the Scriptures teach. You will wrestle effectively against the kingdom of darkness and prove the Scripture that says, "Greater is He who is in you than he who is in the world" (1 John 4:4).

And yet, as we will see, even with these recourses, you will probably still need help in changing your behavior.

QUESTIONS FOR GROUP STUDY
OR PERSONAL REFLECTION

1. If Satan wanted to destroy you—and he does—how would he do it? What area in your life is the most likely place for him to attack? What weakness makes you most vulnerable?

2. Here are the seven pieces of armor listed in Ephesians 6:12–17. Included is a brief description of what each piece ought to mean to us personally.
    a. The belt of truth (v. 14): complete honesty.
    b. The breastplate of righteousness (v. 14): confession of all sin and a constant looking to Christ who is our righteousness (1 Cor. 1:30).
    c. Feet shod with the preparation of the gospel of peace (v. 15): eagerness to present the gospel wherever and whenever possible.
    d. The shield of faith (v. 16): implicit trust in God's Word.
    e. The helmet of salvation (v. 17): confidence in the hope of salvation and the sufficiency of the cross.
    f. The sword of the Spirit (v. 17): knowledge of the specific statements of God to apply at the point of temptation.
    g. All kinds of prayers and requests (v. 18): prayerful attitude of thankfulness and dependence.
What steps do you plan to take to put on any missing pieces?

3. In addition to using Scripture as suggested in the chapter, we must learn to pray against demonic activity in our families, church, and also in specific individuals. We can do this best by putting on the armor of God daily and rebuking satanic activity through the use of Scripture.

A sample prayer might be:

> *Father, we thank You that Jesus Christ has ascended far above all principalities and powers. We rejoice that because we are joined to Him, we participate in His victory. We thank You that Satan and his armies have been defeated and must be subject to our exalted Savior. Now in Jesus' name, we ask that Satan's activity be stopped in the life of _____. We bring the mighty truth of our Lord's victory against all of Satan's workings in _____'s life. We desire to be in fellowship with the Father, Son, and Holy Spirit throughout this day. We offer this prayer to You, Father, in the name of the Lord Jesus Christ. Amen.*

Chapter 12

TRAPPED AGAIN

Hopefully by now you have made some progress in tackling that habit that wouldn't budge. Maybe you've gone a day or even a week without slipping back into the same old sin, so you're probably pretty optimistic that finally you can see the light at the end of the tunnel. You can finally begin feeling better about yourself, right?

Wrong! Be careful here, because this is precisely the moment most of us find ourselves failing again. We think our past is history, and so we let down our guard. But that is just the invitation Satan is looking for to come barreling back into our lives.

So then, should we conclude that we were deluded—that victory isn't possible after all? Heavens no! We should be assured that our victory is most definitely real. But it is not enough to stand up once, only to fall down again.

So what happens to keep us from breaking the cycle for good? Several things, possibly. Jerry G. Dunn, a former alcoholic, discovered a pattern among alcoholics, which he illuminated in his book, *God Is for the Alcoholic*. As I've studied it, I've concluded that all of us experience this cycle in one form or another. Dunn did a lot of research to find out why alcoholics would quit drinking and enjoy a period of abstinence, only to return to drinking. God gave him insight into this problem, and that's when he noticed the cycle, which Dunn says can take a week, a month, or even years to complete.

First, the alcoholic desires never to take another drink. He's had it. Never again will he make a fool of himself—waking up in strange rooms, not knowing how he got there. Just remembering the humiliation of the past keeps him sober for awhile.

Such a feeling is usually the first step toward freedom from any habit. We are tired of gaining weight, losing our temper, or whatever. We become so weary of failure that we begin to seek a way of deliverance. So many Christians haven't even come this far yet! They are still not weary of their sin. Some of the more obnoxious habits may go, but not the subtle ones. Some sinful habits are still too attractive to discard completely. As we've already stressed, God wants us to desire victory for reasons other than personal fulfillment. But usually, our quest for freedom begins with a healthy disgust for our failures.

Second, Dunn noticed that alcoholics begin to take pride in their sobriety. They'll say, "You know, I haven't had a drink in three weeks." The alcoholic begins to feel better—he might even get his job back and regain the respect of his children. Soon he begins to have a superior attitude when watching his friends drink. He thinks to himself, "I'd never act that foolishly again, thank God." Yet it is difficult for him to avoid the constant bombardment of alcohol. Social drinking is accepted, and his friends invite him to join. He is still proud of his abstinence and yet fears that he just might slip back into his former habit. Dunn says, "This is what we call 'a dry drunk.' This man has reached the place where he has to fight against taking another drink. He is disgusted with people who drink. He can't stand the smell of liquor. He becomes irritable, and someone's suggestion that he have a drink becomes a personal insult."

But after enduring the struggle for some time, the alcoholic begins to think he has solved the problems that have caused his addiction. He feels better physically and mentally. Perhaps he has even begun to attend church, so he thinks his spiritual life is in order. He breathes a sigh of relief. At last, everything will be all right.

Finally, when he feels he has mastered the situation—or at last feels he has his problem under control— opportunities to drink become more numerous than ever. One of his associates says, "Aw, you can handle it." Until that point, he has been refusing such offers. But suddenly he feels he is the master of a whole new world. Surely he is able to handle a single drink. So he says yes—just once.

At this point, Dunn says, the alcoholic goes in one of two directions. If he is able to stop at one drink, he confirms his conclusion that he can handle drinking. He loses his fear of alcohol. He finds it easy to take another drink when it is offered. But more often, that one drink re-inflames his passion for alcohol. Dunn writes, "One drink might be enough to plunge him back into the very depths of alcoholism as quickly as one can be pushed over a cliff."

Either way, the end result is the same: He will become completely victimized by the bottle again. Dunn mentions a doctor who completed the cycle in ten years. By drinking half a glass of beer, he started another binge that eventually ruined his home and cost him his practice.

Your problem may not be alcoholism, but my guess is that your cycle follows the same pattern. I know I've gone through the same steps with other sins. Let's take a look now at what we can learn from such failures.

WHAT DOES GOD WANT TO TEACH US?

God uses our failures to teach us several lessons. The moment we fail, we receive a crash course in theology. We are vividly reminded that "pride goes before destruction, a haughty spirit before stumbling" (Prov. 16:18). John Bunyan was right when he said, "He that is low need fear no fall."

Remember the Israelites at Ai? They had just conquered Jericho, a city fortified with huge, strong walls. God had just done a miracle—the walls had collapsed. The next city on their agenda was the smaller town of Ai. Fresh from the victory of Jericho, the men decided that only a small contingent would be needed to conquer the city. But the Israelites were defeated. Their self-confidence was ill-founded. In their enthusiasm for victory, they had overlooked the sin that was in the camp. Their past victory was no guarantee for future success.

We must learn that our most dangerous moment is when we think we have finally mastered our situation. A series of victories sets us up for a fall. Not one of us should ever say, "This is one sin I have under control. I'll never commit it again."

God loathes self-righteousness—a superior, judgmental attitude. How easy it is to say, "I'd never do what *he* did!" Anyone who says that has no idea of what he is capable of doing. There is no sin beyond the capacity of any one of us. If we have not succumbed to the same degree of evil as others, it is because we have not had the same opportunities to do evil, and more important, because God's grace has restrained us.

Remember the Pharisee who went into the temple to pray? He's generally remembered for reciting all of his good works to God. But what we often overlook is that he didn't take the credit for his high moral standing—at least he said, "God, I thank You that I am not like other people" (Luke 18:11). But although he *thanked God* he was not like others, he did not receive God's mercy. Why? Because even good works done in God's name are never the basis for acceptance. The humble tax collector was accepted precisely because he understood that the basis of his acceptance was God's mercy alone.

Even the oft-repeated assertion (usually recited by smug, self-possessed Christians who never seem to struggle like the rest of us), "There but for the grace of God go I," can be said self-righteously. We think we are different, better than others, because we have attracted God's favor. Even such refined self-righteousness is anathema to God. He wants us to see that, in essence, all human beings are the same. If we are objects of His special grace, it is because of His sovereign pleasure; it's not because we are better than others.

Our failures help us learn these lessons. I don't know what Paul's thorn in the flesh was, but it originated with the Devil. He says it was "a messenger of Satan to torment me—to keep me from exalting myself." (2 Cor. 12:7). Yet that weakness was expressly allowed by God to keep Paul from pride and self-righteousness.

God does not cause us to sin, but He uses our sins to remind us of our weakness. We are less tempted to judge others, and more understanding of their failures, when we become well acquainted with the wickedness of our own heart. We then learn how to view others with humility, considering ourselves, lest we also be tempted (Gal. 6:1 KJV). When we are caught by sin, God uses the experience to teach us about His righteousness and His hatred of sin.

God also wants us to appreciate the wonder of His grace. "Where sin increased, grace abounded all the more" (Rom. 5:20). Because of pride, I find it hard to admit that I need God's grace so continually, so desperately. How we would all like to be able to say, "I've not committed that sin in ten years." But our continual problems with sin crowd us to the cross. Again and again, we are confronted with Calvary; we are forced to come with nothing in our hands to receive God's provision freely given from His grace.

Peter summarizes it all for us by saying, "Clothe yourselves with humility toward one another, for God is opposed to the proud, but gives grace to the humble. Therefore humble yourselves under the mighty hand of God, that He may exalt you at the proper time" (1 Peter 5:5–6).

Signposts to Failure

At Niagara Falls, there is a point of no return in the river—a place where the water rushes so fiercely that it would be impossible to make progress against the stream. At that point, going over the falls is inevitable. There are warning signs that tell the unwary where that point is, but some foolhardy souls either have ignored the signs or have not seen them. Most are not around to tell us which it was.

We have our warning signs too. Generally, they're slow leaks and not blowouts that stop us. Failure, actually, is quite predictable. We can tell whether we are on our way to the point of no return.

What are those signposts? The first is a feeling of self-satisfaction, a sigh of relief that finally we have everything under control. At that moment, we are vulnerable because our confidence rests with ourselves and our past record rather than with the Lord. Remember the alcoholic? He thinks he has drinking under control. He must be reminded that he never has drinking under control. Even at Alcoholics Anonymous meetings the participants are trained to say, "I am an alcoholic." And they must remember that fact even after they have been dry for ten years.

Friend, we are sinners. And we will continue to be until the day we die. We must beware of thinking that we have any sin permanently under control. "Don't be so naive and self-confident. You're not exempt. You could fall flat on your face as easily as anyone else. Forget about self-confidence; it's useless" (1 Cor. 10:12 MSG).

Then there is the danger of making a hidden provision for defeat. Dave wanted desperately to overcome his addiction to pornography, but he kept some inappropriate DVDs in his room just in case he was tempted! Or consider the woman who wants to stop smoking but keeps a pack of cigarettes in the drawer, thinking that she might need them.

Our mind is like a huge house with many rooms. We might be willing to clean up the kitchen, the living room, and even some of the bedrooms. But what about the closet crammed with junk? Perhaps it is precious to us for it represents one small part of our life we are not willing to surrender to the searchlight of the Holy Spirit. But Christ wants to be the master of our entire life. Everything that is hidden He wants to reveal. There is only one way we can meet God's requirement, and that is by refusing to keep any room in our life that can be used as a retreat from our spiritual commitment.

God wants us to perform radical surgery on sinful habits. We must burn all our bridges. This is what Jesus taught in the Sermon on the Mount. Immediately following His remark about the sin of lust, He made a shocking statement: "If you want to live a morally pure life, here's what you have to do: You have to blind your right eye the moment you catch it in a lustful leer. You have to choose to live one-eyed or else be dumped on a moral trash pile. And you have to chop off your right hand the moment you notice it raised threateningly. Better a bloody stump than your entire being discarded for good in the dump" (Matt. 5:29–30 MSG).

Once an eye is gouged out or a hand cut off, there is no chance of it being put back. The separation is final; there is no hidden agenda for a comeback. Paul wrote, "Don't loiter and linger, waiting until the very last minute. Dress yourselves in Christ, and be up and about!" (Rom. 13:14 MSG).

There is also a signpost for spiritual coasting. That's what happens when we begin to crowd God and His Word to the circumference of our lives. This happens so subtly as we feel more pressured by the responsibilities of life: jobs, spouses, children, hobbies, church, friends—even TV, the Internet, the newest cell phone....

I've been on a boat that has left the shore so quietly that I scarcely noticed it. That's the way most backsliding happens, slowly and without fanfare. Only tragic failure makes us realize how far we have drifted from the shore. God prefers that we be either cold or hot, not lukewarm (Rev. 3:16). The reason is simple: Someone who is cold seeks fire, someone who is lukewarm is generally comfortable and sees no need for change. He is so self-satisfied that he doesn't know how bad off he is! The believers at Laodicea, to whom these words were directed, were lukewarm but thought they were hot. They had drifted from their first love and didn't even know it. Gardeners tell us that weeds will always take over when we stop growing healthy plants and pulling weeds out by their roots.

Finally, there is a signpost for compromise. That's when we tolerate personal sin for just a little while. I have seen a man shatter a cement wall with a huge hammer. The first time he hit it, the wall was as solid as ever. Even after twenty blows it seemed immovable. But he kept at it. After awhile the wall began to crumble a bit, though it still stood firm and upright. But it was weakening! First one small piece fell, then another, then gradually it collapsed.

That's the way sin is. It is true that we can tolerate sin without having it ruin us—but we can't do that for long. Compromise might sometimes be possible without disastrous results, but eventually it weakens our resistance.

How many Christian leaders have we heard of recently who have become involved in the sin of adultery? Such affairs probably begin innocently enough—first friendship, then a few fantasies and some lustful thoughts. But such escapades of the imagination weaken a person's resistance. Like the cement wall, people—even pastors—can remain solid for a while, believing all is well. But eventually their wall will collapse.

Watch for these signposts. They are warnings for you on your journey. Get back on course and keep your eyes on Jesus, the Author and Finisher of our faith (Heb. 12:2 KJV).

How Long Before You Stand Again?

You've been caught in the old trap; you're back in the same rut. How long should you stay there? Satan would like to say, "Forever. After all, what's the use? Since you're not really sure you'll be victorious next time, why bother?"

You could be tempted to agree. Human nature resents the idea that we must come back to God without an "award for special merit" sign pinned on our vest. We are uncomfortable accepting mercy that we don't deserve. We hesitate to come back immediately without a period of probation. We may even want to appease our guilt by punishing ourselves by withdrawing from God and His people. So we postpone our appointment with the Almighty until we have proved we mean business and that we will never fall again. Furthermore, we argue, guilt is good for us. It will teach us never to do that again!

God thinks otherwise. To think we must straighten up before we come back to Him reveals a misunderstanding of the cross. We are to come solely on the merit of the blood, not on the merit of an acceptable track record. *Guilt is not God pushing us away from Him; it is God trying to put His arms around us.*

So, is guilt good for us? True, it teaches us how uncomfortable the aftereffects of sin can be, but it's doubtful whether guilt is an acceptable motivation to change our behavior. At any rate, nowhere in the Bible do we read that God uses guilt to discipline His children. Natural consequences of sin, yes, for they teach us how reprehensible sin can be. But guilt is not God's means of discipline; it is contrary to the cross. God's method of motivating us to live righteously is His love and grace. Listen to Paul: "So here's what I want you to do, God helping you: Take your everyday, ordinary life—your sleeping, eating, going-to-work, and walking-around life—and place it before God as an offering. Embracing what God does for you is the best thing you can do for him" (Rom. 12:1 MSG). Grace, freely given, does not provide us license to sin. Rather, it should motivate us to give ourselves without reservation to the One who loves us so freely, so deeply. Whenever you sin, God wants you to come back into fellowship immediately. Learn your lessons, but within His forgiveness, not outside of it.

Sometimes we hear that we should keep "short accounts" with God. It's a way of reminding us not to let sin pile up in our lives. Don't think that you have to wait until the church doors open, or even until the end of the day, before taking care of your sin. Confess it the moment it comes to your attention. In fact, don't keep short accounts with God, but keep *current* accounts with God. Whether you are driving your car, working in the office, or doing chores at home, you can be engaging in dialogue with God. As you speak to Him, He replies through His Word.

Listen to the hope of the Scriptures for all who sin:

> Thus says the Lord, "Do men fall and not get up again? Does one turn away and not repent?" (Jer. 8:4)

> God gives a hand to those down on their luck, gives a fresh start to those ready to quit. (Ps. 145:14 MSG)

> Do not rejoice over me, O my enemy. Though I fall I will rise; though I dwell in darkness, the Lord is a light for me. (Micah 7:8)

> No matter how many times you trip them up, God-loyal people don't stay down long. (Prov. 24:16 MSG)

> The steps of a man are established by the Lord, and He delights in his way. When he falls, he will not be hurled headlong, because the Lord is the One who holds his hand. (Ps. 37:23–24)

You *can* say no to that stubborn habit by saying yes to God once again!

QUESTIONS FOR GROUP STUDY
OR PERSONAL REFLECTION

1. Think back to the last time you were trapped by your weakness. Did you have any indication that you were going to give in to the temptation? What can you learn from that experience?

2. In what ways do we sometimes entertain temptation, thinking that we can handle it and know where to stop? What does this type of attitude show about our lives?

3. What do you think might be the best antidote to drifting in our spiritual lives? Or are there several precautions that are needed? Think of ways that we can lessen the chances of spiritual stumbling. Write them down.

4. Why do we often delay our confession of sin after we have sinned? What lessons have we not yet learned?

5. Why do you think sin is so subtle? Spend some time in prayer right now. Ask God to bring to light the areas of your life that need renewal, and thank Him that He has given us that possibility through His Son Jesus.

WRITING THE LAST CHAPTER

You have now read and pondered the basic principles that God can use to renew your mind and change your behavior. Where do you go from here? What can you do to follow through on any commitment you have made?

This book is incomplete unless it is applied; we must not only know the truth but do it. For this reason, you will write the last chapter. Most of us do not need more truth than we already have; what we need is to weave what we know into the fabric of our own daily lives. So here is your opportunity to take over where this book leaves off. You will decide how this book will end in the way you deal with temptation.

To write the last chapter, purchase a thick notebook. It will belong to you alone—no editor will read its contents to see if it is marketable. There is no need to review your grammar or use a dictionary to check your spelling. This chapter is between you and God.

This notebook will become your spiritual journal, a chronicle of where you are in your life, where you want to be, and the steps you will take to get there. Of course, you can write whatever you wish in your book, but I am including some suggestions that you may want to incorporate into your journal.

QUESTIONS FOR GROUP STUDY
OR PERSONAL REFLECTION

1. Write a letter to God, telling Him about your past—the failures and the successes. Be sure to include your weaknesses, or bad habits. Share with God the desires of your heart. Specifically, tell Him what you would like to have Him do in your life during the next five years, the next year, and the next month. Concentrate on character qualities, remembering that His goal is that you be conformed to the image of His Son (Rom. 8:29).

2. Write out special prayer requests for others: your wife or husband, your children, your relatives, your friends. Be specific.

3. Ask God to give you wisdom to outline a strategy to become the person you believe He wants you to be. This will include items such as beginning each day with God, memorizing two or more verses of Scripture a week, learning and engaging in the ministry of intercession for others.

4. Try to anticipate the ways that Satan and the flesh will attempt to prevent you from following through with your commitment, such as sleeping too late, watching TV, being disorganized. Minimize the

possibility that you will fail. How much is a disciplined relationship with God worth to you?

5. Regularly record in your notebook items such as:
    a. specific prayer requests and their answers,
    b. special observations you make about the Scriptures that are of particular help,
    c. the lessons that God teaches you.

Let your book become a monument to God's faithfulness in your life. If you do, the most important chapter in this book will be the last one, the one that you are writing. The apostle Paul acknowledged that the best book is a life lived in the power of the Spirit: "You are our letter, written in our hearts, known and read by all men" (2 Cor. 3:2). May God help you to begin today.

TIPS FOR SMALL GROUP DISCUSSION AND/OR PERSONAL STUDY

After going through each chapter on your own, sit down and go a little deeper. If you are going through this book with a few other people, take some time to get together with them before moving on. Here are a few thoughts on how to make the most of your time.

Set ground rules. You don't need many. Here are two:

First, you'll want to commit, as a group, to see this through to completion. Significant personal growth happens when group members spend enough time together to really get to know each other. It doesn't have to be every week, but you do need to establish some element of consistency to your time together. If you are working through this book on your own, make a commitment to yourself to finish.

Second, agree together that everyone's story is important. Time is probably the most valuable commodity today, so if you have just an hour to spend together, do your best to give each person ample time to express concerns, pass along insights, and be a participating member of the group. Small-group discussions aren't monologues; however, a one-person-dominated discussion isn't always a bad thing either. Not only is your role in a small group to explore and expand your own understanding, it's also to support one another. If one group member truly needs

more of the floor, give it to that person. At times the needs of one outweigh the needs of many. Use good judgment and allow extra space
when needed; *your* time might be the next occasion your group meets.

Meet regularly. Choose a time and place and stick to it. Don't be
surprised if this becomes a struggle. Go into this study with that expec-
tation and push through it. If you are working through this book on
your own, set aside a weekly time and place where you know you will be
able to concentrate.

Let God lead. Each time you get together, guess who else is in the
room? That's right—God. Be sensitive to how he is leading. Does your
time need to be structured? Then following the book's structure is a good
idea. Does the time need breathing room instead? Then take a breath, step
back, and see what God does.

Talk openly. You'll all be a little tentative at first. You're not a bad person if you're a little hesitant to unpack all your *stuff* in front of friends or
new acquaintances. Maybe you're just a little skeptical about the value of
revealing the deepest parts of who you are to others. Maybe you're simply
too afraid of what those revelations might sound or look like.
Uncomfortableness isn't the goal; rather, the goal is a safe place to share
and be. But don't neglect what brings you to this place—the desire to be
known and find meaning for your life. And don't forget that God brings
you to this place—you're not a part of your group by random chance.
Stretch yourself. Dip your feet in the water of honest discussion. Healing
can often be found there. Again, if you're going through this book on your
own, even being honest with yourself can be difficult. But instead of talking openly, try writing frequently. Record all your thoughts and emotions,
and let God do His work.

Stay on task. If structure isn't your group's strength, then try this
approach: Spend a few minutes sharing general comments about the study,
and then take each question and give everyone in the group a chance to

respond. While you're listening to others, write down thoughts that their words prompt within you. When you are asked to pray, listen to each other read prayers aloud. If you're working through this book on your own, simply make sure that your study time is free of distractions. Don't work in front of the TV or while you're waiting for the bus. Honor the changes God wants to make in your life by taking your time with Him in this book seriously.

Follow up. Don't let the life application drift away without further action. Be accountable to each other and refer back to thoughts from previous chapters often. Take time at the beginning of your group's meeting to review and see how you're doing. Pray for each other between times you get together. Call group members who God brings to your mind and simply ask, "How ya doin'?" Once again, if you're working through this book on your own, take the questions seriously. Reach down deep and be honest with God and yourself. It's your best chance at spiritual growth.

BIBLIOGRAPHY

Adams, Jay E. *Competent to Counsel*. Grand Rapids: Baker Book House, 1970.

———. *You Can Sweeten a Sour Marriage*. Grand Rapids: Baker Book House, 1975.

Augustine. *Confessions*. Oxford: Clarendon Press, 1992.

Bubeck, Mark. *The Adversary: the Christian versus demonic activity*. Chicago: Moody Press, 1975.

Christenson, Larry. *The Renewed Mind*. Minneapolis: Bethany Fellowship, 1974

Christians Unite. "Two Great Lies by James Stalker." Articles. http://articles.christiansunite.com/article9614.shtml (accessed August 2, 2007).

Dunn, Jerry G. *God Is for the Alcoholic*. Chicago: Moody Press, 1975.

Kiev, Ari. A Strategy for Daily Living. New York: Free Press, 1973.

Shelhamer, E. E. "Traits of the Self-Life." Harrisburg, VA: Christian Light Publications, 1994.

Spiegelberg, Nancy. "If Only I had Known You." Godthoughts, http://www.godthoughts.com/only.htm (accessed August 2, 2007).

Meyer, F. B., qtd. in Guido, Michael. "The Book of Acts: Message Three." Guido Gardens Online. http://www.the-sower.org/acts/03.htm (accessed August 2, 2007).

RESOURCES

STEPS TO PEACE WITH GOD

1. RECOGNIZE GOD'S PLAN—PEACE AND LIFE

The message you have read in this book stresses that God loves you and wants you to experience His peace and life.

The BIBLE says ... For God loved the world so much that He gave His only Son, so that everyone who believes in Him may not die but have eternal life. John 3:16

2. REALIZE OUR PROBLEM—SEPARATION FROM GOD

People choose to disobey God and go their own way. This results in separation from God.

The BIBLE says ... Everyone has sinned and is far away from God's saving presence. Romans 3:23

3. RESPOND TO GOD'S REMEDY—CROSS OF CHRIST

God sent His Son to bridge the gap. Christ did this by paying the penalty of our sins when He died on the cross and rose from the grave.

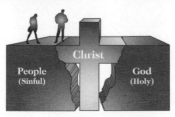

The BIBLE says ... But God has shown us how much He loves us—it was while we were still sinners that Christ died for us! Romans 5:8

4. RECEIVE GOD'S SON—LORD AND SAVIOR

You cross the bridge into God's family when you ask Christ to come into your life.

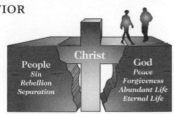

The BIBLE says ... Some, however, did receive Him and believed in Him; so He gave them the right to become God's children. John 1:12

THE INVITATION IS TO:
REPENT (turn from your sins) and by faith RECEIVE Jesus Christ into your heart and life and follow Him in obedience as your Lord and Savior.

PRAYER OF COMMITMENT
"Dear Lord Jesus, I know that I am a sinner, and I ask for Your forgiveness. I believe You died for my sins and rose from the dead. I turn from my sins and invite You to come into my heart and life. I want to trust and follow You as my Lord and Savior. In Your Name, Amen."

If you are committing your life to Christ, please let us know!
Billy Graham Evangelistic Association
1 Billy Graham Parkway, Charlotte, NC 28201-0001
1-877-2GRAHAM (1-877-247-2426)
billygraham.org